PRAISE

"A wonderfully, heartwarming book! Each story is designed to pro-
voke a reaction—a laugh, a chuckle, a smile, a tear. Written in an
easy-to-read, down-to-earth style, you can read this book all in one
sitting, or read a story a day. Either way, this book lives up to its
promise—it WILL make you smile."

—Lisa P. Lubbock, TX

"His knack for finding the heart—serious or funny—of a situation kept me enthralled with every story! I highly recommend it to
everyone who has a heart or a funny bone!"

—Eileen P. Junction, Colorado

"This is one of my all-time favorite books. Bo's stories transcend
education, economy, and age. Each one generates distinctive
thoughts and emotions and can spark remarkable conversations.
This is certainly not just a book for veterinarians or for those who
live in small towns."

—Emily B., Davis CA

CROWDED

in the Middle of

NOWHERE

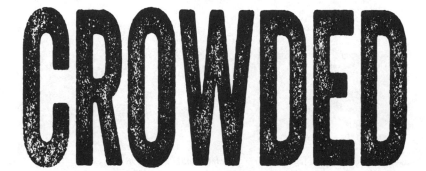

CROWDED

in the Middle of

NOWHERE

TALES OF HUMOR AND HEALING

— *from Rural America* —

Dr. Bo Brock

Veterinarian

GREENLEAF
BOOK GROUP PRESS

The names and identifying characteristics of persons referenced in this book have been changed to protect their privacy.

Published by Greenleaf Book Group Press
Austin, Texas
www.gbgpress.com

Distributed by Greenleaf Book Group

For ordering information or special discounts for bulk purchases, please contact Greenleaf Book Group at PO Box 91869, Austin, TX 78709, 512-891-6100.

Cover design by Main Street Designs, Inc., Pinehurst, N.C.
Interior design and composition by Greenleaf Book Group
Cover photo by Ashton Graham

Cataloging-in-Publication data is available.

Print ISBN: 978-1-62634-264-4

eBook ISBN: 978-1-62634-265-1

Part of the Tree Neutral® program, which offsets the number of trees consumed in the production and printing of this book by taking proactive steps, such as planting trees in direct proportion to the number of trees used: www.treeneutral.com

TreeNeutral

Printed in the United States of America on acid-free paper

16 17 18 19 20 21   10 9 8 7 6 5 4 3 2 1

Second Edition

CONTENTS

Otis, or Why I Became a Veterinarian

At two days post graduation, I wasn't the surest diagnostician to answer a farm call. I was off to my first case—on my first day of work—and my first foray into being a real vet. As I drove to the ranch, I ran through the possible causes of the symptoms that the man had explained to me over the phone.

Crossing the fifth cattle guard after the sixth turn through the rough county around Clarendon, Texas, I saw Otis standing at the foot of a steep cliff. I had never met him before, but I quickly noted that he was a type-B fat guy. You know the kind I am talking about: He wears his pants *below* the belly. The type-A fat guy wears his pants *above* the belly, and those pants usually have a zipper that must be twenty inches long. (You male readers know what I mean: When you're standing at the urinal during football half-time and you hear a zip that lasts about two seconds, you know it's either a coat unzipping or the type-A fat guy with a twenty-inch zipper.) Otis, I would learn, always smoked a cigar and had the vocabulary of a sailor.

"Where is she?" I asked after climbing out of my truck. He pointed up to the top of the fifteen-or-so-foot cliff to a small, flat spot where the cow had collapsed and lain down. We climbed up the side of this dry riverbed together, him huffing and puffing, and me wondering what the heck this cow could have wrong with her.

When we arrived, I saw a huge Shorthorn cow lying on her side and paddling her legs. She had been paddling for so long that she had dug wedge-shaped trenches beneath her. I began to feel the sweat roll down my neck as I pondered what in the world could have caused this behavior.

Otis asked, "What in the hell could be wrong with that big ol' cow, young doctor?"

I had no idea. I needed to stall for as long as possible and collect my thoughts. I told Otis I had to get something out of the pickup and slid back down the bank. I decided the best thing to do was to get some blood and see if lab tests could help. With blood collection tubes in hand, I scurried back up the cliff to the cow and her big, fat owner.

Much to my surprise, when I stuck the needle in the cow's vein, the blood ran chocolate brown. Wow, what luck! They had taught me about this in veterinary school. The cow had nitrate poisoning from grazing the milo (sorghum grain) patch across the creek. And guess what? I actually knew how to help her!

The next trip down the cliff to my truck found me walking with a spring in my step and even whistlin' a tune. I gathered up the anti-dote and scurried back up the cliff.

Otis was impressed with my confidence and even smiled for a second. "So, doc, how long till she gets up after you give her this stuff?" he asked.

To this question, I had no answer. The text books don't give you that kind of information; they just tell you how to treat the problem. That's why they call it the *practice* of medicine, and at this particular moment, I was practicing on my very first patient. I gave Otis the standard I-really-don't-know answer: "It varies from animal to animal." There are just some things you learn as you go, and I was going to learn how long it would take the antidote to work.

I gave the cow the medicine in her vein and, to my surprise, she hopped right up! In fact, she hopped up and looked mad. She looked real mad. First, she looked at me, then she turned to Otis. I guess she decided that he looked easier to catch and softer to head-butt because she went running at him with mean intentions.

I did what any valiant veterinarian would do in this situation: I ran down the hill and jumped into the back of my pickup. I thought Otis was right behind me—and the cow was right behind him—but he wasn't. She had him cornered on that little cliff, and she was whoopin' him.

At first, I was amazed at his agility. For a fat guy, he was putting some moves on this cow. But that only lasted for a short while. You see, she was still a little uncoordinated and stiff from being down so long, but that only took about three or four charges to get over, and then she had her youthful athleticism back. On the fourth pass, she got him. She rolled him like a rubber ball to the cliff's edge, and then with one mighty shove, over he went. Good thing dry creek bed sand is soft, because I really think I saw Otis bend backward so far that his head touched his fanny.

"Are you OK?" I shouted from the safety of the truck bed.

"S---, no!" he screamed back at me.

"Well, you better get well quick," I said, "because she is coming down that cliff with a bad look in her eyes!"

At this, he leaped—all three hundred pounds of him—out of the sand and rushed toward the truck. I noticed that his stride was getting shorter as he approached me, but I wasn't sure why. It looked like the cow was going to reach him before he got to safety.

I screamed, "Run faster! She's catching ya!"

In the heat of the chase, his butt-crack-baring pants had slipped down to just above his knees, making it impossible for him to throw a leg up over the side of the truck. He got to me before she got to him, but he was too tired to jump into the truck. As I was trying to pull him in, I grabbed anything I could get ahold of. In this case, that turned out to be his size-fifty-two boxers. Basically, I was giving my very first client a wedgie.

Otis, cigar still in place, assessed the situation and bent down to pull up his pants. This left him only enough time to run to the other side of the truck to avoid being rammed by the charging-at-full-speed cow. Once again, I was amazed at his speed. He managed to stay ahead of her as they played keep-away around the truck. Each time he came by, I would offer him my hand and tell him to jump for it. But each time he thought she was too close, and he would back out at the last second and make another lap.

Finally, at the hood of the pickup, on about the sixth lap, she caught him. His pants had come down again, and his stride was just too short to outrun her. Otis was taking about fifteen steps per yard there at the end, trying to avoid her rush. But it was to no avail. He rolled up into a big ball, and that cow bounced him around and through everything in sight. I jumped out of the truck and did the best rodeo clown imitation that I could, but she was determined to roll him for awhile before she came after me.

But, just as suddenly as she had come up from that dose of medicine, she quit and strolled off. When I got to Otis, he was covered in stickers and cow patties. His hat had been smushed flat. His shirt was torn in several places. His pants were down around his ankles, his giant boxer shorts were full of dirt, and he was cussing a blue streak. But he never lost his cigar, nor did it sustain even a bit of damage.

I learned three things on my first farm call. One, if you're a type-B fat guy and work with cattle, you better wear suspenders. Two, when you got a cow down from nitrate poisoning, you had better head for the truck as soon as you give it the antidote. And, three, there are some things you just can't learn in school, like you might have to give your first client a wedgie.

I knew on that day that I was in for a great career.

———

I was twelve years old when I realized I wanted to be a veterinarian. I have always considered myself lucky to have found my calling so early in life. I have seen so many talented people wrestle finding something that interests them and struggle to decide what they want to do. But, from the age of twelve, there was never any doubt for me.

It happened on a hot, early August evening—the experience that persuaded me to become an animal doctor—when Lucy, the only sow on our farm, was having her babies. Let me tell you, this was a big deal to twelve-year-old me. I had fed and taken care of that sow every day that she had been alive. She might have been just a pig to most people, but she was my four-hundred-pound buddy.

I was there to see Lucy pop out her first baby. I was amazed by the entire process and couldn't wait to see how many she would have and to have a herd of little piggies to take care of. As the second one slid out, I was more amazed than ever. I pulled the afterbirth off the piglets and gently shook them. They immediately got up and headed for milk. I was totally entranced by birth and all that it included.

But something went wrong with the third one. Lucy strained and grunted, pushed and moaned, lay down and got up, but nothing came out. I knew there had to be more than two. What in the world could be wrong? I ran into the house and got Papaw. I told him that Lucy was having her babies, and the third one wouldn't come out.

Papaw ambled out to see what his young grandson was going on about. He looked at Lucy and made some of those "hmmmm" sounds that old men make when they are thinking. After a few minutes, I could tell that he had concluded that I was right—Lucy, sure enough, had a piggy stuck.

Papaw went to the barn and came back with a slick substance that I had seen him use when delivering calves. He smeared it all over his arm and hunkered down behind Lucy. I watched her eyes get big as Papaw's arm slid into her birth canal.

It seemed like ages passed before he finally said, "That piggy is coming upside down and backward, Turdhead. I am gonna have to put a lot of pressure on it to get it out. It ain't gonna be pretty, so if you want to go in the house, now is the time to do it."

No way! I thought. There was no way I was leaving at that moment. I told him I was gonna be there no matter what; I could take it.

He went to work trying to reposition the piggy and get it out. It was a painstaking process, and I could see him wince every time she would have a contraction and smush his arm. The minutes passed, and I could see sweat building up on his forehead. I didn't know whether to feel sorrier for him or her as they both worked hard to bring life from inside her.

Finally, he got that rascal out. The piglet was huge, way bigger than the first two, and dead. It was just another moment in my childhood that confirmed that my granddad was a hero. He could fix anything, as far as I was concerned, and this was simply proof of that assumption.

He set the dead piglet aside and told me to stay there and see what happened next. I wouldn't have left for anything, and the fact that he trusted me to be the sentinel just made me more determined to see it through to the end.

About fifteen minutes passed, and Lucy began pushing again. Nothing. Ten more minutes, and all sorts of juicy stuff came out, but no piggy. I ran back in the house and told Papaw of the new developments.

What we saw when we returned to her pen absolutely floored me. Lucy had prolapsed her rectum and vagina pushing out the next piggy. It was the most awful thing I had ever seen. But Papaw took it all in stride, like it was somethin' he saw every day.

He simply went back into the house and returned with some of Mamaw's thread and a tickin' needle. He pushed everything back inside Lucy and sutured her up. He told me that she was gonna die and that I needed to make sure her two piggies sucked as much as they could before she passed on.

I just couldn't believe it. Why did she have to die? Was there just nothing on earth that we could do to save her? I couldn't accept that my pig was gonna die because there was nothing we could do to fix her.

Papaw's prediction came true, of course. Lucy died the next day and left me with two orphan piglets and a lot of questions. I decided then and there that I needed to learn to fix stuff like this. I was certain that Papaw could have done it if he only knew how. That conviction never left me.

You might be wondering how all this rambling has anything to do with a fat guy named Otis. Well, it has everything to do with him.

Fourteen years had passed between the moment I told Papaw I was gonna be a veterinarian so I could fix things like what had happened to Lucy and the day I headed out to do just what I had promised I would do. It just so happened that my first call would be for a cigar-smoking, type-B fat cowboy and his poisoned cow on a dry creek bed near Clarendon, Texas.

I can vividly remember thinking about Lucy and Papaw as I drove the twenty miles to meet my first clients. I can remember the emotion of thinking I had finally made it and was a real doctor. I had gone through that vet school with a determination few others could muster because I was driven to fix every sick animal I encountered for the next forty years or so.

And I actually fixed that cow. She certainly would have died if I hadn't come into her life. I'm really proud of that. But I still feel the irony of how that first animal tried to dismember her owner, and I have contemplated the significance of that irony ever since.

I knew on that day with Otis that I was in for a great career because I realized that many of the lessons Papaw instilled in me as I grew up were more important to being a good veterinarian than all of the science I learned at Texas A&M vet school.

After twenty-four years in practice, I still believe that is true.

———

I left Clarendon, Texas, in January 1992 to start my own veterinary practice in Lamesa, Texas. When I left, a fella there told me, "Lamesa is in the middle of nowhere. You will never be an accomplished veterinarian there. You'll be an outstanding horse vet in Lamesa when pigs fly!" You can imagine why that fella was one of the main reasons why I wanted to leave the Texas Panhandle for a West Texas town of approximately ten thousand residents.

When I got settled in Lamesa, the local paper asked me to write a monthly article about veterinary-related things. That is what happens when small towns in West Texas need copy for their newspaper. I wrote the first couple of columns about important veterinary topics like parvo in dogs and why you should get a Coggins test for your horse. Can you believe that no one read them? So, I decided my third attempt would be something a little more humorous about being a rural veterinarian. This—yes, this—made all the difference!

As fate would have it, a reader had a relative who was a veterinarian in another state and decided to send the story to him. He liked it so much that he sent it to a veterinary magazine up north. They liked it, too—enough to give me a call. The fella at the magazine asked me if I wrote that type of article often or if it was the only one

I had composed. When I told him about my local newspaper gig, he said he'd love to publish an article a month in the veterinary magazine. I have been writing about the moments in life worth describing ever since.

I thought about naming this book *When Pigs Fly* but decided that that title might be a little misleading, because I've never made a pig fly. So, I decided on *Crowded in the Middle of Nowhere*. After all, it is the story of being a veterinarian to more than 25,000 clients at the edge of the earth and loving it.

Crowded in the Middle of Nowhere is a collection of the most notable moments. My Papaw, Elmo Brown, is responsible for instilling in me a keen perspective on the world. I remember listening to him tell stories at the dinner table, recounting to my grandmother what he and I had lived through together during the day. Listening to Papaw's observations, I quickly realized that I was not paying close-enough attention to everyday life, and it set me on a lifelong mission to discover how he perceived the world. I will be forever grateful to Papaw for loving me and teaching me to see the special moments that happen right in front of us every day.

I hope this book touches the depths of your emotions. I hope you laugh, I hope you shed a tear or two, and I hope you discover how wonderfully blessed we all are to share our lives with animals and appreciate every smile they prompt.

— *One* —

Family

I wonder what being me would be like without the group of close-knit people that make up my family. I'm older now and most of them have passed on, but I see them so differently now than when I was young. They were all I knew as a kid. I guess I just supposed that every family, everywhere, was just like ours, only with different bodies. But I was wrong. My family was its own unique group of characters, the likes of which I haven't seen since.

I watched them work and learned my views of the world and values just by being with them. They were all so diverse and different, yet they all operated with an unspoken motif: happiness and laughter. They all were funny people. They taught me how to find the funny side of life, and they taught me how to appreciate laughter by respecting crying, and disarming anger.

Seeing your children grow up is an amazing thing. I watched them be born, and I took them to college and cried when I left them. I spent my young adulthood focusing on how to instill the same values in them that all those old people had instilled in me, which means I am the old guy now. I have had more laughs, more tears, more fear, more anger, and more emotion over all from them than anything life has offered.

This collection of family stories is first in this book because I wanted to share where I came from and how I wound up in the middle of nowhere. Before I go off on yarns about the life of a veterinarian, I want to give a little introduction to how the values of rural America were instilled in me from my earliest days and how I have tried to instill it in my babies.

Nonny

My grandmother, Nonny, grew up in a family of five sisters and one brother. She and her siblings shaped me and gave me my perspective on life. They were rural, moral, salt-of-the-earth people who held firm to their beliefs and spent their entire lives honing their keen senses of humor.

This moment in time starts with my great-uncle J. W., the lone brother in the family, making a trip to the booming city of Amarillo, Texas. While his wife was undergoing some tests at a hospital there, he would stay with two of the sisters, my Nonny and Jo Anna.

For as long as I can remember, Nonny and Jo Anna were naggers. They weren't mean or ugly, just a little hardheaded, and if something wasn't just how they thought it should be, they would tell you about it over and over until you fixed it like they wanted. Every time I saw them, they would nag me about my moustache, or my constant wearing of a cap, or me working too many hours. They would harp on it endlessly, until it almost drove me crazy.

J. W., a farmer/rancher who didn't come to town very often, had arrived in Amarillo with his truck bed full of the tools of his trade: a saddle, some wrenches, a few bits, some plow shanks, and a saw or two. When Nonny and Jo Anna saw the state of his pickup, the nagging began.

"J. W., you better lock that stuff up before you go to the hospital or someone'll steal it. You ain't in Brice. This is the big city, and people are just aching to take stuff like that."

The nagging continued even as his climbed in the cab and drove out of the driveway. I am sure after growing up with this bunch, he had learned to let it go in one ear and out the other.

The sisters, arriving at the hospital a little while later, found J. W.'s pickup in the parking lot. They parked next to it and checked the doors. Sure enough, he hadn't locked them. And all his stuff was still piled in the truck bed just waiting to be pilfered. Being the crafty women they were, they decided to take matters into their own hands by putting all his tools in their trunk. That would show J. W. not to leave all his stuff unattended in the big city.

How I wish I could have seen those two old women shuttling all that stuff out of J. W.'s truck and into their trunk. It must have taken them thirty minutes! Some of that stuff was heavy, but they managed to move every bit of it before heading inside to check on their sister-in-law.

Saying nothing of what they had done, they visited with J. W. and his wife, giggling to each other for no apparent reason and exchanging sly smirks. They were just waiting for him to discover his empty truck and learn his lesson about taking their advice to "lock them things up."

About an hour later, one of the sisters noticed that the pickup they had parked next to was gone. (The window of the hospital room conveniently looked out on the parking lot.)

"Why, J. W., someone stole your pickup," Nonny said as she gazed at the empty spot next to her car.

Unconcerned, J. W. strolled to the window. He said, "No, they didn't. I parked over there, next to the fence."

Nonny and Jo Anna's faces went white. They looked like two little girls who were about to be sent to the principal's office. Their trunk now held all the tools from some other country bumpkin's pickup—and he was gone. How would they ever find him to give all that stuff back? Worse yet, what if he came back with the police and they found all of that stuff in *their* trunk?

I laugh hard every time I think about that moment. They actually called the TV station and asked them to put the event on the six o'clock news so that whomever they had robbed could get his stuff back. The TV station declined, so they had to call the police, explain the entire humiliating event, and hand the stuff over.

Nonny died on the last day of 2005. She was over ninety and still just as feisty as she was the day she robbed some cowboy of all his tools. We miss her deeply.

Mamaw

Even though my Papaw was a farmer/rancher, my Mamaw would iron his work clothes every day. I could never understand why. Most days, Papaw never saw anyone but me and maybe a few other crusty farmers.

Mamaw mixed up her own starch in a glass Coke bottle topped with cork/metal cap that had a multitude of holes in it, like a salt-shaker. She would sprinkle Papa's pants with the starch, and hang them over a chair for a few minutes so they could dry a bit, and then apply the heat of the iron to them.

Because I watched her do this through my childhood, I considered it normal. I just figured that every old woman in the world did it—it was all I had ever known. But, as the years passed, I began to question this practice. Why in the world did Papaw need his work clothes ironed? Mamaw never ironed my clothes, and there was no way I saw any use in doing it for myself. Heck, my clothes were usually so dirty by 9:00 a.m. that any sign of ironing would be long gone.

One day when I was about thirteen, I asked Mamaw about it. I wanted to know why she thought it necessary to invest time and effort pressing clothes that were rarely seen and would be filthy in just a short time.

Her reply was as sweet a sentiment as I have ever heard.

She told me that Papaw was the most handsome man in the world. She said he was her best friend and the love of her life. She loved every chance she got to show him off and make the rest of the world jealous that he was hers. She went on to say, "You just never know when Papaw might run into someone, and I want him to look the part of the most handsome man God ever made."

I looked closely at Papaw later that day. He sure didn't look all that handsome to me. He was a short, skinny man with a relatively big fanny compared to his shoulders. His hair was thin on top, and his false teeth didn't line up too good when he smiled. He wore horn-rimmed glasses that were much too big for his face because all he cared about was being able to see. I really didn't see how anyone could consider this man the most handsome one God ever made.

So, I asked her about it a few days later. I informed her that I had closely observed ol' Elmo Brown and most certainly didn't see him as the most handsome man on earth.

She giggled and gave me a girlish smile that grandmothers just shouldn't be able to express at that age.

"You just aren't looking in the right light, Turdhead. He is the most beautiful man God ever made. Those eye wrinkles haven't always been there. I remember when he had real teeth. He has the most beautiful blue eyes I have ever seen. They are exactly the same color as the sky just before the sun goes down. His entire face lights up when he smiles, and his voice is so calming and full that everyone in nine counties wants to hear him talk."

Say what? My Papaw had always been an old man as far as I was concerned. I never knew him any other way. Was Mamaw actually wanting me to consider that Papaw used to be young? Ha ha ha ha, no way!

She continued, "I want him to feel beautiful! I iron his clothes every day because for all these years, he has made me feel beautiful.

He is a man worthy of respect. I want him to look the part every day. I wouldn't have it any other way."

I heard what she said and was kinda grossed out. It was ridiculous to me, and I just decided to forget I had ever asked. How could this old woman think that an old man with false teeth was beautiful? *Old people . . . sheesh*, I thought.

I watched Mamaw and Papaw grow old together. I was probably thirty when it dawned on me what beauty really was—it was Mamaw ironing Papaw's pants with starch from a Coke bottle, and she taught me how to see the world that way.

Papaw

"Good throw!" Papaw shouted as I completed my first back-of-the-pickup rope sling.

I caught the sick calf around the neck on the first attempt and, at twelve years old, no words could have made my head swell bigger than that kind of "atta boy" from him.

I called my grandfather "Papaw," and he called me "Turdhead." He was my hero. He had the patience of Job as he taught me how to whirl a rope and size my loop. He taught me to keep the slack until just the right moment when I could close the loop down on my target.

It has been a while since he died, but just today I remembered him deeply with the fond memories that come only after the sting of loss has passed, revealing the voice he left to guide me. It was his voice I heard with each item I removed from the trailer.

My wife, Kerri, and I finally got a barn out beside our house so that I could move the things Papaw left to me out of storage. The day after Papaw died, I loaded up all the things in the barn that he had told me would be mine when he passed and packed them neatly into the stock trailer that had belonged to his dad. The trailer and all my treasures had been in storage since a few days after he died.

It took me hours to move those pieces of our shared history from the trailer to the barn. Each nugget brought back a moment that he and I had spent together, of Papaw teaching me, and me not even knowing there was a lesson in progress. He made learning the lessons of life such fun that it wasn't until years later—long after I had grown into a man—that I realized how much he had taught me and how much time he spent doing it.

As I dug through my treasures, I uncovered a bottle of Thermic Liniment. It must have been thirty years old. He used it on every sore horse we ever had; he said it "pulled out the swellin'." Papaw could fix anything that was ailing, and he was especially particular about how to care for our animals. Everything had to be done correctly and at the right time. Even though he was just caring for the animals in his charge, he gave me an incredible passion to care for critters that lives on today.

He would often ask me what I thought the horse I was on might be thinking. He would tell me that if I would look at things through the horse's eyes, it would open up an entirely new world. Through the eyes of critters, I would find an entirely new perspective.

———

"Good throw!" Papaw shouted as I completed my first back-of-the-pickup rope sling around the sick calf's neck. The thing he hadn't told me was what I was supposed to do next. The calf may have been sick, but he still weighed five hundred pounds, and I only weighed in at about eighty-five. I watched as the coils of rope in my hand got smaller and smaller and the calf got farther and farther away. In a panic, I dallied to the nearest thing in sight, a CB antenna coming off the truck's headache rack. Well, the antenna had broken off years before, and all that remained was the spring that made up the base. This, of course, was not going to slow down that calf.

As the tension reached the spring, the knot on the end of the rope hit my hand. Not wanting to disappoint my hero, I held on to that knot for dear life. The next thing I heard, as I went airborne, was Papaw's voice: "Let go of the rope, Turdhead!" He was saying it over and over, and the sound was getting softer and softer as the calf pulled me in the direction of his momma. By now, letting go was not an option. The bracket of the antenna had wedged between my hand and the rope, and I was being pulled along like a rag doll.

The only thing I remember hurting while I was being pulled was my left ear. I must have been surfing on that ear for about a hundred yards before any other part of my body hit the ground. The dragging began to slow as the calf wore down and he approached his destination, stopping just short of his momma.

Being twelve years old and made of rubber, I hopped right on up and jumped on the calf like I was a rodeo clown. By the time Papaw got to us, I had the calf tied up and was working him over.

If you can tell how bad a dragging is by the amount of dirt in your underwear, this had been one monumental drag. I had enough earth in my britches to grow potatoes! As I got up to walk away, gravity took control and it filled up my boots.

I miss Papaw. I miss his view of life. I miss being called Turdhead. I wish I had told him how much he influenced me and how I watched him and hung on his every word. I'm grateful he was alive to see me become a veterinarian, a mission that he instilled in me through his own example.

In his own way, Papaw displayed how proud he was without ever saying those words. I wish he were here now to read how the words he spoke to me as we rode through the weeds and mosquitoes gave me a whole new perspective. I wish he were here now to give me the guidance I still need and to fill my world with his thoughts, but I guess I'll have to settle for the voice he left to guide me.

More Papaw

There are just some things that make a difference in your life—things you will never forget—but you may not realize how important they are when they happen. This moment was one of those.

My dad died the year before I started vet school, and all the money my mother had for the rest of her life was a measly life insurance policy. I had worked hard to have enough money to pay for that first year of vet school. I knew I wouldn't get much financial aid because that life insurance policy made it look like my mother had made a huge amount of money in one year, disqualifying me for grants or loans. By about three-quarters of the way through that first year, I was broke. I mean really broke.

I was so broke, I lived on oatmeal and rode a frickin' moped to school because I couldn't afford to get my truck fixed. I had saved enough money through high school and college that I thought I could get through that first year, but by March I was running out of funds and my stress level was high. I was so tired. I had been studying hard for days and trying to deal with being totally without money. I was wondering if this would ever pay off and how I was gonna make it through three more years.

Papaw called me one Monday night. He hated talking on the phone, but he must have known something was up. We small-talked for a few minutes when he suddenly asked me how much money I needed. Say what? How could he know that I was in a money crunch? I had not told a soul about my moped riding and oatmeal eating.

I told Papaw that things were pretty tough. I told him that I wouldn't ask my momma for money because she needed what she had for the rest of her life. What he said next hit me right in the heart. He told me not to worry, that he would have some money to me by Friday and that I should eat some beef or something that was not just oatmeal. He laughed about the moped and told me to use the money he was sending to get my truck fixed. I told him I needed about $1,000 to make it through, and then I would get a job for the summer. He had a calming way and I knew things would be OK.

Papaw's check arrived with the Friday mail. In the envelope was a check for $10,000. *Ten thousand dollars!* It was the single largest check I had ever seen, and it was made out to me.

I had worked with this man all of my life. He had paid me like a hired hand, and I had always had everything I needed. I never asked for money, and he never offered it. I had worked my way through college and bought my own truck and horses. But just then I was holding a check in my hand that said more than any dollar amount. It said, "Bo, I believe in you. You're gonna make it, and I am proud of you."

When I finished that semester with a 4.0 grade point average I sent him my report card and told him that he was my hero.

I will never forget how that burden left my shoulders and my spirits lifted when a check from an old, West Texas cowboy came in the mail. Papaw's faith in me gave me a strength that I will never forget. It was an amazing moment.

My Mamaw later told me that he put my report card in his truck. She said he showed it to everyone in the county anytime he had the chance. She said she had never seen Elmo Brown brag about anything in her life, but he bragged about his grandson every day. That knowledge was worth much more than $10,000 to me.

Stinky Dad

Do you remember what made your father special? Perhaps it was the sound of his voice when he whispered good night, the way his footsteps sounded across the floor as he approached your room, or the look on his face that meant you'd better straighten up.

Or perhaps it was the way he smelled in the morning when he hugged you before leaving for work. It was probably just his shaving cream, cologne, or deodorant, but it was a fresh, dad scent. Depending on what your father did for a living, the fresh morning scent might have sharply contrasted the smell he came home with at night.

I hadn't realized how conditioned my children had become to the rituals of life and my own dad scent until one evening when I returned from work to find a houseful of eleven little girls, between the ages of four and nine and all talking continuously, over for a slumber party.

I immediately went to work on the tent that we were to pitch atop the trampoline, with the help of five or six of the girls. Can you think of anything cooler than sleeping in a tent on a trampoline?

Emili, my oldest daughter, was next to me, holding the things needed for assembly. She hugged me and told me she was glad I was her dad. Soon, another girl stood next to me to hold a rope. I noticed she had a huge frown on her face and was holding her nose.

When I asked her what was wrong, she replied, "You stink, bad."

Funny, Emili had just hugged me and hadn't complained. I chalked it up to the girl having a soft-nose and went on with the tent assembly. But a minute later, I noticed the same look on another helper.

"What's wrong with you?" I asked.

"I don't mean to be rude, Mr. Brock, but you smell worse than anything in the world," she said.

I decided it was time for a little research. I walked over to my middle child and gave her a pick-up-and-swing-you hug. She smiled and hugged me back. Not a word about my aroma.

Then, I went to Kimmi, my youngest, and did the same. Again, not a mention of any BO (no pun intended).

Some of the other girls thought the spinning hug looked like fun and wanted to take a turn, but when they came down from the spin, most commented on how bad Abbi's dad smelled.

Admittedly, it had been a stinky day. Pigs, postmortems, cow palpations, abscesses, and who-knows-what-else had been on the agenda. And with the temperature nearing one hundred, I'm sure my whole staff acquired a layer of perspiration. Absorbing the pungent odors one at a time, my nose didn't register them. But that didn't mean they hadn't clung to me.

That experience made me reflect on my girls' lack of reaction to their stinky dad. They probably think that every father comes home smelling like a carcass. It probably even comforts them—here comes Daddy, home from work, smelling like manure. Everything is right in the world.

I began to think about other conditions they consider normal that their peers probably don't. They can pick up blood-soaked gauze and never bat an eye. They have seen more shots given than most people see in their whole lives. They have even helped me do C-sections on cows.

I am sure there will be a time that having a stinky dad will be a huge embarrassment to them. But, when that phase passes, and they become grown-ups with kids of their own, I know they will find a strange degree of comfort in the smells of an animal hospital.

They Do Listen to Songs

Kerri and I have three daughters, and I have always been amazed at what goes through the minds of children. They notice things in their world and they store those moments. Then they bring them up at the strangest times.

One Friday, the phone rang at about 11:00 p.m. It was Dr. Marty Ivey from Ruidoso, New Mexico, with a colicky horse that appeared to need surgery. The critter would get to Lamesa around 3:00 a.m. I told him to send it on, and we would be glad to try to make that horse happy again.

The carrier arrived at the expected time and unloaded a very sick racehorse. We got the horse in the stocks, and after an extensive examination, I told the horse carrier that surgery would be the only option. The exam revealed a twisted gut. This is not a good thing for a horse. Surgery is about the only option, and sometimes even that offers little hope.

"This is a very special horse," the road-weary man muttered. "I sure hope you can fix it."

Every horse is a "very special horse" in the eyes of someone. I understand that, and treat them all as though they are the most important horse in the world.

"This horse belongs to Toby Keith," the carrier muttered in his exhaustion.

I immediately imagined an interview on repeat all over Country Music Television, with my picture in the background complete with stupid look on my face. Toby Keith tells the interviewer: "Yeah, that's him. That's that vet from Lamesa, Texas, who killed my prized racehorse." Worse yet, what if Toby and Willie Nelson wrote a song about "the redneck vet from West Texas" who couldn't save a horse from a bellyache? What if it became a hit and played on for generations? The stakes were high and the pressure was on.

I gathered my crew and we did the surgery, just as we have on hundreds of other horses. It went well, and I felt fairly optimistic about the horse's condition when we finally left the clinic on Saturday evening.

When I arrived home, I gathered my three girls to tell them that I had just saved Toby Keith's horse. You see, they were huge fans and had all his CDs. I just knew they would have a few "wows" for my triumph.

Much to my surprise, this is not what I heard from my eight-year-old, Kimmi.

"I knew that was going to happen," she said matter-of-factly, like she had been expecting it for some time.

What in the world would elicit this reaction from an eight-year-old? How could she ever even imagine that Toby Keith's horse would wind up in Lamesa, let alone at her dad's vet clinic? She had heard about many colic surgeries but never one on a celebrity's horse. Kerri and I sat there for a moment with wondering looks on our faces when Kimmi broke the silence.

"Yeah, I knew that was going to happen; you're not supposed to give beer to horses."

Our puzzled looks quickly became mouth-open, eye-squinting laughter.

Kimmi, having heard Toby's song "Beer for my Horses" many times, figured it was just a matter of time before one of the singer's horses developed gut problems and would need to go see her daddy.

Kimmi's older sisters, Emili and Abbi, chimed in, "He didn't really give beer to his horse; that is just a song."

"No, it's not," Kimmi fired back. "Why would he say it if he didn't do it?"

Toby's horse recovered well and went back home to New Mexico. We never heard from him personally, but as far as Kimmi was concerned, I should have called him and informed him that whiskey for the men might be OK, but he'd better stay away from giving beer to the horses.

And there you have it: the mind of a child. I love it.

What Kind of Heinie?

Because my daughters were growing up with a mixed-animal veterinarian for a father, I figured they had seen just about every anatomical part of a mammal. But my youngest girl, Kimmi, who had spent all of her four years with two sisters, her mother, and six girl cousins, had never been exposed to human "boy parts." Finally, we had a boy cousin. Kimmi was four years old when the little tyke came to the house to spend a few days.

As Kimmi sat in the big chair watching television and eating Cheetos, my wife plopped the infant boy on the floor to change his wet diaper. I looked across the room just in time to see Kimmi's focus shift from cartoons to the now-half-naked baby. With her head cocked to one side—like a dog hearing a high-pitched sound—she developed a curious expression as the Cheetos consumption came to a gradual stop.

She slid off the chair, licking one hand clean of the neon orange Cheetos residue and the other grasping the half-empty bag. She made her way to the baby and bent at the waist to get a closer look.

It is always funny to me to watch a little kid process new information. This was not the normal anatomy, and she knew it. I could feel the smile growing in the corner of my mouth and could hardly wait to see what she would do next.

Kimmi just stood there, still licking cheese powder off her hand, and watched as Kerri cleaned and readied the baby for a new diaper. Several times it looked as if she was about to say something, but the thought never gained enough organization for her to form a sentence.

Finally, after several minutes, she cut her eyes to Kerri and said, "What kind of heinie is *that*?"

Not wanting to miss an opportunity to be a father, I replied, "That's an evil heinie. You stay away from heinies like that!"

She looked at me with a puzzled, almost terrified look and backed away from her baby cousin, almost as if he would jump up and attack her.

Like a good mother, Kerri clarified for Kimmi, and we laughed about it for days. But the funny moment made me think a bit about having three daughters and what an adventure it is going to be when boys come courting. The more I thought about it, the more it worried me.

Someday, *boys* were going to want to date *my* three beautiful girls. What was I going to do? Well, I composed a sign and put it over the front door:

CAUTION

I'VE CASTRATED THOUSANDS OF ANIMALS.

IF YOU WANT TO DATE MY DAUGHTER,

DON'T BE AN ANIMAL.

Fishing

It was a Saturday afternoon, and I was fixin' to take Emili and Abbi (my two oldest daughters) fishing. In West Texas, going fishing is a huge undertaking because there aren't any fishing holes close by. So, when a family in Seminole opened a fishing pond, it sounded like the kind of fun I wanted my girls to experience.

I spent days telling them about fishing and showing them how to cast and bring in the line. I told them that if we caught any catfish, we were gonna fry them up and have them for supper. I couldn't wait to show them how to clean and cook a catfish. We were all looking forward to the adventure.

As a solo practitioner in small-town America, I should have known better than to look forward to anything. Just as we loaded the last fishing pole in the truck, the phone rang. A cow C-section was on the way in to the office. How do you explain to two little souls that their fishing trip is off because Daddy had to go work on a cow?

They were both understanding, as usual. They had never known anything different. Daddy was always having to leave and go in to the clinic to work on som'in' sick. They had just come to expect it. But this time it really irked me! I was totally excited about taking them fishing.

I explained to them that as soon as I was done working on that cow, we would head to the fishing hole. I decided that if we couldn't fish now, we would later, and I would even let them suture the incision on the cow to make up for the delay.

The cow arrived at the clinic exactly one hour later than the grumpy ol' rancher said it would. He unloaded her and hollered at me that he was going home; he had plans with his family. Man, that just made things even better.

The girls and I loaded the angry cow into the chute. She wanted no part of humans and she was gonna whoop anything that got in her way. Can't say we really blamed her. When we finally got her into the squeeze chute, she promptly laid down. There is no way to do a C-section on a cow in that position. She needed to be standing, or rope tied and lying on her right side so the incision can be made in her left flank. We were in a mess.

I explained to the girls how to tie her feet and restrain her so we could help her and I went about getting the ropes around her feet and legs. Then we gradually opened the side gate to the squeeze chute. The cow must have decided that she couldn't give birth without our help and finally allowed us to go to work on her. We calmed her down and restrained her as I explained to the girls why the calf was stuck. I let them both put a palpation-sleeve-covered arm into the birth canal so they could see how the calf was twisted up and much too big to come out that way.

I am not sure how much they understood that day, but they will surely remember this poor cow when they have kids someday. They were both completely focused on getting that calf out of its momma.

As I considered what my girls would learn from assisting in the C-section, I remembered asking my momma what the f-word meant after a boy in my third-grade class had been sent to the principal for saying it. My momma told me that the two dogs that had been "stuck together" on the back porch were doing that, and that it was how animals made babies. I grew up thinking that someday I was gonna get "stuck together" with a woman that way in order to make a baby. Reflecting on that made me really aware of what my girls would take away from this event.

I explained to them how we would get the baby out. I also explained how it got in there in the first place. I described the difference in skin thickness between cows and people. I told them about a uterus and an ovary. I told them how sperm coupled with an egg. I did all this without ever saying any of those grown-up words and while we were actually getting that calf out of the predicament it was in. They never even knew I was teaching them a thing.

I let them make the incision through the cow's tough skin. I told them how lidocaine killed pain. I talked about how muscles made an animal move. I showed them the stomach after we got in and told them it's where food goes when they swallowed. I taught them about sterility while we shaved the cow's hair and scrubbed her side with iodine.

I watched their faces as we pulled a living calf out of the cow's uterus, helping God bring new life into the world. I told them how the baby had been surrounded by fluid and got its blood from the momma through its belly button so it didn't need air until it was out on its own. I hung the calf upside down to drain the fluid from its lungs and had them help it breathe by suctioning the fluid out of its nose and mouth. My kids were completely consumed in the moment of birth. They were building a memory that would influence their essences and color their imaginations for always.

They were young, but ready. It was amazing to me how my five- and seven-year-old were so in tune to the introduction of a new life. I spent a few minutes considering how everything was new for them. It was a thought-provoking realization that they would remember this moment, which they shared with me, for their whole lives.

We finished, and everything went well. As we cleaned up and washed away all the stuff that comes out when a baby is born, I noticed that Emili had a spot of blood on her white tennis shoe. I asked her why she hadn't cleaned it off.

She replied, "I'm gonna show that to everyone at school on Monday. Lots of kids that can go fishing with their dads, but I'm the only kid around that got to deliver a baby calf with my daddy this weekend."

I thought about her statement so often. Many veterinarians say that their careers have kept them from having any time with family. They gripe and complain because they can't go fishing often enough or take vacations. And I agree, being a vet can be overwhelming.

But, oh my, have they ever missed opportunities to let their children take part in some of the most wonderful moments that life has to offer. Like Emili said, anyone can go fishing on a Saturday afternoon. But how many kids get to help Daddy bring a new being into this world and watch it take its very first breath?

Pucker

I grew up watching my grandmother quilt. She sewed every evening. I would watch her and think how cool it looked for her to slip that needle through the cloth with the aid of a thimble or two. She would tell me that I needed to be practicing on cloth so I would be ready for skin when I became a veterinarian. So, she'd let me help her put a "blind hem" stitch in the patterns of the quilt. I did it for hours in the evenings as I grew up. She made it look so easy; all the pieces were precut and fit together so well. I figured that the only difference for a vet would be that suturing is on tissue, but I was well on my way for a veterinary education.

Soon after becoming an animal surgeon, I realized that tissue seldom goes together as nicely as precut patterns do. If you are doing an elective surgery, such as a spay or neuter, where you make the incision yourself, then sure, the skin edges go back together just like the patterns on those quilts. But if you are repairing a horse that ran through a fence, or the shreds of a dogfight, the pieces tend not to fit just right.

To get an idea of what I mean, cut a circle in a paper towel and see if you can sew the thing back together; or, better yet, try attaching a garden hose to an inner tube.

The end result of suturing things back together that don't fit is a pucker. When one side is longer than the other is, a pucker results as you approach the end of the cut. The question is what do you do with a pucker? Over the years, I have faced them countless times, and they are considerable adversaries.

A pucker just sticks out, begging for some attention. Most of the time, the owner is standing there, peering over my shoulder with that look on their face that expresses a complete lack of confidence.

I've even had people ask me, "What in the world are you going to do with that *great big pucker* that is forming as you go?"

I have overcome my fear of puckers in the last year or so. We have developed a five-step approach to handling them. If there is someone in the room with you, say the next sentence aloud for full appreciation of its melody.

"You can poke a pucker, tuck a pucker, pleat a pucker, dart a pucker, or cut a pucker. We go through this series of remedies, and we quit when one works."

We start by poking the pucker with one of our suturing instruments. It should disappear beneath adjacent skin, and if it doesn't leave too big of a bump or come out when you shake it, then you are done.

If the bump is too big or the pucker bulges when you shake it, then you should try to tuck the pucker by putting a stitch over it to hold it underneath the surrounding skin. If that works without leaving too much of an ugly pile of skin, then you are done.

If pucker tucking is unsuccessful, then proceed on to the pleat technique. Simply take one big pucker and make a bunch of little puckers out of it. They're a little like pleated pants: They lie flat but have room to expand. This works well and can be quite cosmetic. If it works, then quit; you are done.

But some puckers are too stubborn even for the pleat technique. These require the assistance of scissors. The pucker should be grasped with a pair of forceps while you remove a neat wedge of skin. The *V* that is left in the skin then can be sutured together to form a nice, neat *I*. All but the most treacherous of puckers can be defeated by this dart-a-pucker procedure.

The frustration level gets a tad high if this procedure doesn't work, so we come to the last resort: cut a pucker. Grab the thing; cut it off, and walk away before your blood pressure gets any higher. I would not recommend this technique in front of squeamish clients.

Oh, I forgot to mention what is perhaps my favorite variety of pucker. Our girls call it the plant-a-pucker; it's what Kerri and I put on their rosy cheeks every night as we tuck them into bed.

Two

West Texas Ingenuity

When it comes to the public . . . perception is reality.
—Dr. Chuck Deyhle, 1991

West Texas is more than just a place, it is an attitude. It's where friends will say "We're fixin' to have y'all over this weekend." I didn't know that West Texas was anything other than the way the entire world was until I went to Texas A&M University to attend veterinary school in 1986. I met people there who broadened my cultural understanding and opened a new, different, and exciting world to me. But as my time at A&M passed, I realized that I am a West Texan, and I belong in West Texas. So, I came home.

West Texans are ingenious. They can fix anything with a spool or even a scrap of baling wire and a roll of duct tape. They can conjure something useful from nearly nothing and adapt to difficult conditions with a smile and a handshake.

Stories of West Texas ingenuity demonstrate how West Texans think. The people are racially and culturally diverse, but they have so much in common that their differences seem to be insignificant. They all seem to think the same, have the same views, watch the same television shows, and eat way too much red meat.

We are all products of our circumstance and our surroundings. I hope these stories will give you a taste of the culture of the region stretching west of Abilene.

Never Put a Pig in Your Mouth, and Other Wise Things Granny Taught You

The first Thanksgiving after I graduated from vet school brought my two grandmothers, my "city girl" sister, my mother, and my brother for a visit.

As the newest vet, I was on call every weekend and holiday because everyone else was tired of not being home enough. And, as is always the case when you have special plans, the phone rang at 8:00 p.m. It was a woman from a town about forty-five minutes away with a gilt pig that was not having luck delivering. She informed me that this was no ordinary litter of piglets. The daddy of these babies was the greatest of all pigs, and he had died since this batch was conceived. If we didn't get a little boy pig, his genes would be gone—forever. No pressure.

Of course, my entire family wanted to go observe the pig situation. My grandmothers were just "so proud" of their grandson. No one in my family had ever finished college, much less gone for eight years. They thought I could do no wrong and wanted to see me in action.

We met the pig's family at the clinic. The owner—a tall woman with a gruff voice—was wearing an EMT outfit, including a stethoscope and a pocket protector with all sorts of medical equipment. This turned out to be a vital indicator of the evening's events. She was all business.

My grandmothers were right in there helping and assisting. One grandmother was about five feet tall and weighed about 180 pounds, while the other one was about six feet tall and weighed about one hundred pounds. Boy, did they make a pair! And they weren't alone. My mother, sister, and brother were all in attendance, as well.

As I reached my gloved arm into the pig I realized that there was no way those piglets were coming out the normal way. I told the EMT woman that we would have to do a C-section. She looked even more serious and reminded me that her world-famous boar hog had died. No pressure.

My grandmothers were both in the background saying, "He can do it. He's the best vet in the world." Eeeeeh, no pressure.

I prepared the pig and cut her open. Once inside, I could feel that there were only three babies, and I conveyed that information.

"Well, one of 'em better be a live boy," the EMT said.

Really, no pressure at all.

I pulled out a dead female. The next piglet was another little girl, and she was not doing very well. One left—one chance at a boy. The tension mounted as I struggled to get the last piglet out. Much to my relief, it was a boy. But he wasn't doing well, either.

Suddenly, the EMT woman swooped in and grabbed the piglet from my shaking hands. She rushed it over to the counter and began giving chest compressions. My grandmothers watched intently.

The EMT counted aloud, "a one, and a two, and a three," as she gave chest compressions with her first two fingers. Then she picked up the piglet, stuck his entire head in her mouth, and began blowing.

The next few moments happened in slow motion for me. My grandmothers were aghast. In unison they made that disgusted grandmother noise. I'm sure you've heard it—it's kinda like a cross between a Tarzan yell and a high-pitched yodel. It's the noise they made when you did something gross like pick your nose or spit ice back into your Coke.

My "city girl" sister was retching over the sink while holding her hair back so as not to get anything in it. My mother was saying, "Oh my goodness," over and over. My brother was laughing.

Amid the chorus, the EMT finished her CPR and slapped the piglet back onto the counter to began chest compressions again. My grandmothers leaped into action. One wiped afterbirth off the woman's cheek, while the other said, "You shouldn't put a pig in your mouth!"

Just as they were about to get her clean, she put the piglet in her mouth again. This brought another disgusted-but-harmonious grandma yell.

I could hear them saying, "Oh, honey, you just shouldn't put a pig in your mouth!" They graciously offered to go to the store and get her a toothbrush.

The pig lived. The owner was happy. But my grandmothers would never be the same.

What Do You Do with a Goat in the Kitchen?

When the doorbell awakens you at 1:00 a.m., it takes a few minutes to get your brain to work.

When I heard it ring, my first thought was the alarm and I reached over to hit the snooze button. When snooze didn't work to silence the noise, I realized the dinging noise that had corrupted the extreme quiet of the night was not my morning alarm.

I fumbled with my britches as I stumbled down the hall toward the front door. I pondered the doorbell as I approached the living room half dressed.

"That thing never sounds so loud during the day," I whispered to no one in particular as the obnoxious sound pierced the night again.

Much to my surprise, I opened the door to a man, a woman, six children, and a pregnant goat. They greeted me with wide smiles.

"Our goat is having trouble delivering," the man stated in a concerned, but matter-of-fact tone. "Will you see if you can help her out?"

I ground the sleep out of my eyes, and stepped out onto the porch to assess Tiny, the pregnant goat. In other circumstances, she fit her name completely. She was a little bitty goat in stature, but in her present, very pregnant state, she was as big around as she was tall. And she needed a hand.

I went to the pickup for a palpation sleeve—really, an elbow-length glove—and some lube. As I reached in to see if the babies were about to be born, Tiny let out a bone-jarring scream. It sounded for all the world like a screaming child and all I could think about was the neighbors. What were the neighbors going to think with a noise like that coming from next door?

It looked like my only option was to invite them in and deliver the baby goats in the house. I would have liked to have piled them all in my truck and taken them to the clinic, but I did not think Tiny would make it if we didn't do something fast.

I had felt enough when palpating Tiny to know that those babies were going to have to come out by cesarean. It was one o'clock in the morning, and I was about to deliver baby goats in my house under the watchful eyes of a family of eight. The garage was out of the question due to countless piles of junk from our recent move. It would have to be the kitchen. Kerri would kill me if I got blood on the floor, so I spread newspaper, several layers thick, over the kitchen floor and went to work. Fortunately, I had enough equipment in the vet box of my pickup to do the surgery.

I laid Tiny down, clipped and scrubbed her giant belly, gave her proper anesthesia, and then noticed that one of the six children was standing on the kitchen table. I decided to ignore the kid and focus on helping Tiny.

Every slice with the scalpel brought a chorus of "oohs" from the spectators. They were asking questions about the surgery faster than I could answer. Remember, it was only about ten minutes earlier that I was fast asleep, not even dreaming about doing a C-section, let alone doing a C-section on a goat in my kitchen while a kid danced on the table and his family asked more questions than Alex Trebek on *Jeopardy*.

I got the first baby out and handed it off to one of the parents to dry it off with the only thing I could find, one of my T-shirts from the laundry room. Drying off the next baby took all the paper towels on the roll. The last baby was dried off with two dish towels and a pair of dirty socks that had come off that evening with the T-shirt. I used my daughter's little blue snot-sucker thing to clear the fluid from the babies' mouths and throats.

So far, everything was going well. The babies were all alive, and Tiny was doing fine. It was then I noticed that the commotion had brought Kerri from the bedroom. Picture this: the woman of the house, in her robe, hair pushed into messy piles on the left side of her head, puffy eyes from awakening from a deep sleep, standing in the kitchen doorway with one eye on the four-year-old standing on the table and the other on the goo that was flowing across the newspaper-covered kitchen floor. She was, no doubt, trying to imagine why in the world she married a veterinarian.

I felt a lump in my throat as I tried to conjure up a story of how this all had happened. Just as I was about to explain, a chorus of thanks resounded from the entire family as the children held the baby goats with love in their eyes.

The faint smell of goat in the house lasted for a couple of weeks. Kerri trashed the T-shirt and socks, and I had to mop the kitchen several times to get up the goo. If any neighbors heard the scream, they kept it to themselves. The footprints on the table came off in time, and Tiny went on to have several more litters of baby goats.

Frustration

Have you ever had one of those days when everything that happens just grates on your nerves? You know, those days when even the things that should make you smile kinda make your teeth grit behind your forced grin? Well, when those days come upon me, I think back on the most frustrated critter I have ever known, and it seems to make whatever is irking me seem so incredibly small.

We called him Gomer because that's what he was. During the

process of embryo transfer in goats, we must know when the female is in the right stage of heat to accept the embryo. In order to find this out, we need a male goat that must fulfill a few essential requirements. First, he can't be too big. We don't want him to hurt the females or ourselves. Second, he must be intact so that he can detect a female goat in heat. Third, and most importantly, he must not be able to inseminate the female. So, how is one to accomplish all these things?

Years ago, someone came up with the great idea to create a gomer goat. This is done by surgically moving his "boy part" so that it exits to the side instead of straight ahead. This allows the gomer goat to fulfill all of the requirements. He remains intact but cannot get the female pregnant.

So, I went about making one of these creatures. The surgery is not difficult. After the procedure, we give the gomer about two weeks to recover before putting him to work. The gomer wears a harness between his front legs that has colored marking chalk on it so that when he mounts the female, he will color her back and miss her "girl part." This is how we know which female goat is ready to be used in the embryo-transfer procedure.

I must say, using a gomer goat is a very good idea and works extremely well for everyone involved—except the gomer. You should have seen the look on our poor Gomer's face the first time he mounted a prime female specimen and felt his "boy part" miss the mark. Not only that, but you should have seen the look on the female's face when she realized what was happening.

Gomer hopped off and just froze. I think he suddenly realized why he had been hitting himself in the ear with urine for the last two weeks. He looked to one side and then to the other. I think he was checking to see if he had two. He jumped into the air and then ran about, making a tremendous mad goat sound. He went over and butted a couple of young males as if to punish them for his misfortune. And then, as if he thought perhaps he had merely had a bad dream, he tried the female again.

The result was the same. He just stood there and looked at it. I swear he turned to me, thinking "Can you believe this, Doc? Of all the bad luck. I went to sleep, and when I woke up, my 'boy part' was pointing east. What am I going to do?"

———

As the breeding season went on, we eventually had to check the goats every day. This was a difficult task. A fellow in the clinic one day watching us suggested that we get a dog to help round them up. I told him that ol' Gomer wouldn't put up with a dog in his pen.

The man replied, "That little goat couldn't hurt my dog."

So, I said, "Alright, bring him in."

And he did.

By this point in the season, Gomer was beyond frustrated. He had tried every way possible to work around his problem. He would stand on one foot, mount her from the side, put both front feet on one side, even lie on his back. He would try to talk the female into moving her fanny over. Nothing worked for him. At times, he'd be surrounded by thirty or forty females in heat, and all he could do was mount and watch. His frustration grew until he was just down-right mean.

When this fellow showed up with his dog, it was quite a sight to behold. The dog took off like a shot when he was commanded to get the goats. He ran around to the back of the herd and right into Gomer. Ol' Gomer tore that dog up like a sow's bed. He hung his horn under the dog's collar and carried it around, butting it on everything in sight. The dog yipped and screamed and, for just a moment, I thought I saw Gomer smile.

We no longer needed Gomer when the breeding season came to

an end, so we moved his boy part back to the normal position. I have often wondered if he is still alive, happily breeding nannies. I wonder what he tells the billys down at the barbershop about the season he spent in Lamesa?

Frustration, An Epilogue

Brock Veterinary Clinic has a group of loiterers, a club made up mostly of retired farmers, military dudes, and schoolteachers, and a few people who just come down on their days off to hang out and watch.

I'm not sure how or when this group got started, but it evolved into almost always having one member at the clinic. Very few moments in the day passed without one or two of them standing around watching for what might happen next. Sometimes they get in the way, but most of the time, they just hang back and give commentary on what is going on.

This bothers some people, but it really doesn't bother me too much. I like to hear their old war stories and what they might say about whatever it is that may be happening.

The membership hit an all-time high the year Gomer lived at the clinic. These old dudes thought that was the funniest thing they had ever seen. They would show up in the mornings with lawn chairs and coffee and sit outside the pasture watching poor ol' Gomer swing and miss. It brought a roar of laughter from the geriatric section every time.

They never seemed to tire of watching the process and seeing what Gomer was going to try next to get things to line up. About twice a day, they'd find me and tell me about the latest position Gomer had tried. They absolutely loved it. I often wondered if it was because none of their "boy parts" worked anymore and they could relate to a poor ol' billy goat that just couldn't get the job done.

Having the dudes keep watch turned out to be a really good thing for me. By the end of the day, they could identify every nanny in heat and tell me how long she had been standing. I sure as heck didn't have time to stand there all day and make sure the marking chalk was accurate in showing which critter was ready to receive an embryo. We did a really good job of embryo transferring because of those old rascals.

Screw Down Juice

"Where is that young veterinarian? I need to have a word with him! He gave my horse a shot of screw-down medicine, and I didn't know it!"

I was in the other room, but I recognized the voice—Skeet Black. He was a seventy-eight-year-old ranch foreman, who had retired about five months earlier after having been foreman on the same ranch for fifty years. And I knew that the young veterinarian he was wanting was me.

I had been a vet for only about three months, and things weren't coming easy. Seemed like there'd be weeks when everything I tried just went wrong. I was having one of those weeks when Skeet's very distinctive old-cowboy voice broke through the quiet of the small-animal surgery room where I was spaying a dog.

The spay wasn't going very well. As I worked the four-year-old, overweight, in-heat Labrador, I was beginning to think I would rather have jock itch myself than spay dogs. Everything that could possibly go wrong in a spay was going wrong, and now I was distracted by an old cowboy who was obviously mad at me about something. I hadn't even seen him for a month. What could I have done to his horse that took an entire month to go wrong, and why did he have to come in hollering at the very moment I was grappling with my amateur surgery skills?

Screw-down medicine? What the heck was he talking about? I had been outta school only a few months, but I'd had about 350 hours of college, and I had never heard of screw-down medicine!

I tried to recall what I had done to his mare. Oh yeah, Skeet had retired and decided to take up team roping. He bought a twenty-two-year-old mare—a seasoned head horse—and he was roping with some of the locals. He had brought her in because she wasn't coming out of the box fast enough and wasn't turning quick enough to face the cow. I remembered it well.

My attention momentarily switched back to the fat, bleeding Lab. I was so frustrated with spaying fat dogs that I forgot about Skeet for a moment—until his next words penetrated the quiet surgery room.

"You say he is doing a surgery? Well, I am just gonna wait right here till he gets done. I need to have a word with that fella, and I am not gonna leave until I do."

His voice rang with aggravation and bordered on mad. Apparently, I had given this screw-down medicine to his mare, and something about it had ticked off the old rascal.

I wracked my burdened brain for what I had done to his horse. All I did was inject her hock joints with some triamcinolone. She had bone spavin (a form of arthritis) in those hocks, and I just wanted to give her old joints some relief so she could carry this seventy-eight-year-old fart up and down a roping arena without any pain. I figured the injections would make her feel better and go faster, and everyone would be happy. I had done it on horses before, and everyone seemed to like it . . . apparently not ol' Skeet.

I finally finished up the wretched spay and knew I would have to face him shortly. I had no idea what he was gonna say or why I was in trouble. My stomach was in knots, almost like when I was sent to the principal's office in the fifth grade for doing something for which elementary-school turdheads needed a swat or two.

Let me paint a picture for you of what I was about to face: Just outside the door stood a man who had been a ranch foreman for fifty years. When he brought in his mare, he stood in front of me, rolled a cigarette, and smoked it. He had ridden horses for so long that his forty-or-so-inch inseam was permanently bowed. He wore long-sleeved shirts with those snap buttons when they were completely out of style. His cowboy hat was so ancient and weathered that the brim had rolled up like a taco, and the sweat ring extended to the crown. His boots came to a point, and the leather was so worn that it was as thin as the skin on his giant earlobes. And, to top it all off, he sounded as if he was furious with me.

I finally worked up the courage to open the door to the surgery room and face ol' Skeet. I was still shaking with aggravation from the terrible time I had just had spaying the dog. When I opened the door, I couldn't believe what I saw.

There was cowboy Skeet in a pair of Nike sweatpants and house shoes. He was leaning over a walker that was seven inches too short for his long, lanky frame, and he didn't have his false teeth in, which made him look ninety-five instead of seventy-eight.

"There you are, you young veterinary rascal," he said as he saw my figure appear in the slowly opening door.

"Let me tell you som'in', young'un. I don't know what it was that you gave my mare, but it made her feel so good that she left me in the box when she took off. You told me to stay off her for three days and then start roping again. Well, I did, and that critter took off so fast that I just flew over the cantle of that saddle, bounced off her butt, and landed a-straddle of the fence around Lester's roping arena. Doctor said I was lucky to have balls left after that spill. Now I gotta hip that is aching and have to walk along behind this walker thing for a month.

"I just come in to tell you that you better tell people to 'screw down' after you give one of them there shots. I'm tellin' ya, that critter can run fast and fart loud. Now don't you forget it!"

———

That conversation took place nearly twenty-five years ago, and if you ever come to the clinic with a horse that needs its hock injected, don't be surprised if I tell you, "Now, when I give this, you better screw down, 'cause this rascal is gonna run fast and fart loud!"

U-Haul

I was the only veterinarian at the clinic on a busy day when Boog Peacock called about a "cut-up" horse. He was frantic and his voice rang with worried tones. The horse had gotten into a fence and lacerated a front leg in several places. Ol' Boog wanted me to leave right away and make the drive to his place in Memphis to suture this horse back together. It was an easy, thirty-mile journey from Memphis to Clarendon. I had made the trip along the nice four-lane highway many times. The drive wasn't the issue. The problem was, I was slammed; I couldn't just up and leave.

It was the veterinarian's dilemma: Do you make one person mad, or do you make eight or nine people—who are already at the clinic or on their way—mad?

I told Boog he'd have to bring the horse in. He said he couldn't because he had no trailer. I told him to borrow one. He said none of his friends had horses or cows. I told him he was just going to have to figure something out because it'd be hours before I could make it.

Morning turned into afternoon, and I had forgotten about Boog. When you're a recent graduate, each case takes all of your concentration. It was about four o'clock when an elderly cowboy showed up at the clinic with a horse. He had made the trip from Memphis and was telling another client about the strange sight he had seen on the drive in to Clarendon. I was only half paying attention when I glanced across the parking lot as a blue, '75 pickup truck pulling a flatbed U-Haul trailer pulled in. It was exactly what the cowboy had described seeing on the highway.

Some scenes are just too amazing for words. My mouth fell open as I watched Boog pull into the clinic parking lot with his horse standing on the flatbed, its halter tied to the trailer nose with what looked like about six feet of baling twine.

That poor horse was standing with its legs spread as far apart as a horse can manage. His eyes were wide open and his eyebrows were rounded, making him look like those folks in the photos they take of you plummeting down a giant roller coaster at Six Flags. His tail was tucked between his legs like a scared-to-death dog. His mane stood straight up, electrified by static electricity. His nostrils flared as they slowed to a stop; I figured this was probably the first breath he had taken since Boog broke sixty-five miles per hour.

The horse didn't so much as twitch as the pickup came to a stop. It was as if he was frozen solid. I examined the lacerations and decided to suture the horse on the trailer. There'd be no way we'd get him back on it if we unloaded him. I didn't even sedate him; I just put a local block on the skin to keep the sutures from hurting and went to work. Occasionally that horse would look down at me as if to say, "Would you please buy me from this man so I don't have to ride this thing back home?"

By the time I had finished, there must have been twenty-five people standing around watching. It doesn't take long for news like that to spread in small towns. Everyone wanted to get there in time to see Boog and his rented U-Haul head home. Boog pulled out of the parking lot at 5:30 p.m., heading right on back to Memphis.

———

I wondered what I would have done if my horse was cut up and I didn't have a trailer. I'm pretty sure I never would have thought of hitchin' my horse to a flatbed.

Pappy Can Run

"So, Doc, don't you think it would fix everything if we removed just one of his testicles?" I looked at the stallion's owner, wondering if he was kidding or if he really thought it could happen.

The question surfaced at the end of a detailed story about how his studhorse, Pappy Can Run, just wasn't getting many bookings. With a name like that, you'd think that everyone would want to breed his mare to him, but it just wasn't happening. He'd only had eight mares booked to breed to ol' Pappy in the last season. After long hours of consideration, Pappy's owner was sure he had figured out why.

Seems that four of the twelve mares Pappy had bred the year before last had aborted twin foals. As bad luck would have it, three of the eight mares Pappy bred last year had also aborted twins. I have to admit that the odds of that happening are astronomical, but it was also just bad luck.

But there was no convincing Pappy's owner of that. And not only would he hear nothing of bad luck, he had come up with a solution.

He never considered that the real reason Pappy wasn't booking mares was, well . . . he just wasn't a very nicely put together stallion. He was a little swaybacked, kind of short in the pastern, and a bit jug-headed. He had a poor slope in the shoulder and a left front leg that was a mite crooked, but most of all, Pappy couldn't run. He was slower than molasses. I guess that fellow loved Pappy so much that he just couldn't see the horse's shortcomings, so it had to be something else.

That "something else" was the twinning problem. Yep, that had to be it. Because in this fellow's eyes, Pappy was the perfect racehorse stud. It had to be that the owners of all the really fast mares were afraid that Pappy was throwing too many twins.

He had also arrived at a solution. Yes, he had deliberated endlessly on how to solve the twinning problem. His solution was at the heart of the question. That's right; a stud with only one testicle would ensure that all future breedings to Pappy Can Run guaranteed a *single* live foal.

Tooth Lady

As a consultant veterinarian at a feed yard, you entrust the health program of thousands of cattle to a group of people who are referred to as "doctors." They are not really doctors; that is just the term used by the people who work at the yard to describe what they do. It is the consultant's job to train these people to treat sick cattle, and it can be a frustrating task. Here is an example of why.

Dan Thompson and I arrived at the feed yard at around 6:00 a.m. This particular feed yard used two young women as the doctoring crew. They were not the brightest of individuals, which makes the task of teaching them complicated "doctoring" terms even more difficult.

One of the girls was sitting on a table with a twisted look on her face. The expression seemed to reflect a mixture of disgust and pain. I couldn't really tell which, so I approached her and began asking questions.

It seemed that her boy, Junior, was having problems in school. In fact, they had held him back in the third grade, and considering that it was February, this must have really upset her.

"He's not a dummy. I'm telling you, those stupid teachers just don't know how to teach someone with an IQ as high as his. My momma told me that Junior is just so smart that he gets bored with the slow pace they set over at the elementary school," were the words that came rolling out of her mouth as she began describing the unfortunate events of the last few days.

The expression on her face just didn't seem to match the emotion that should have accompanied her telling me about the "stupid" people over at the elementary school. No, it was something more . . . something almost painful. Suddenly she reached up and cupped her chin with both hands. A mild moan trickled from that same corner of her mouth, and she winced a bit.

"Besides all that, I have a toothache, and it is killing me!"

Dr. Thompson quickly chimed in. "Well, why don't you go to the dentist?"

"I hate dentists. They scare me, and they are all stupid. It got to hurtin' so bad last night that I just pulled it myself."

"You mean to tell me that you pulled your own tooth?" Dr. Thompson squealed, his eyebrows arcing higher on his forehead. "How did you do that?"

"I just got a pair of vise grips and started wiggling it. It must have tooken about an hour of serious wiggling before I got it out. I even had to get my husband to hold my head down because my neck got tired."

"You've got to be kidding! You mean you actually pulled your own *tooth*?" Dan asked as the anticipation of what happened next began to build. He went on to request an examination of her mouth. Sure enough, there was a giant gap about two or three teeth back on the upper left arcade.

"How come it still hurts so bad if you pulled it out?" Dan asked.

"Well . . . I pulled the wrong one. Turns out the one that really hurts is the next one back."

So, you tell me: how far do you think the apple fell from the tree? How would you feel about entrusting the health of millions of dollars' of cattle to this gal? Furthermore, how would you like to be responsible for teaching her?

Tattoos

Tattoos have become quite popular these days. At Texas Tech, where I teach, about one student in three sports some kind of artwork.

But what do you think the folks at the tattoo parlor would say if you asked them to tattoo a pig?

The pig in question was supposed to have a dark-colored nose with a red overtone. It wasn't supposed to be pink.

When the owner put the piglet next to a heat lamp that was too close to the ground, and it burned a large spot on the end of the animal's nose. As the pig grew, the spot turned pink. Pink just isn't acceptable in the show pig world.

My task was to tattoo the nose with something that would restore the correct color.

Just to be clear: I am not a tattoo artist. I don't have anything that even resembles a tattoo instrument. I told the owner he'd have to call a tattoo artist because I had no way of doing it (and really didn't want to be known to have tattooed a pig's nose, anyway).

He asked if I would sedate the pig if he found someone to do the job, stating that the pig was going to get a nose tattoo one way or another and that he'd prefer it be sedated for the procedure.

He borrowed our telephone directory and pulled out his cell phone. I listened as he explained the situation to several tattoo art-ists in the area. Most hung up or laughed so loud I could hear them through the receiver from across the room.

So, no one around was willing to tattoo a pig's nose? Go figure!

But three days later, the owner called to say he'd found the right tattoo artist. He made an appointment to bring in the pig for seda-tion and tattooing.

I was mortified. What kind of guy would tattoo a pig's nose? And who would want to be tattooed with that machine after it poked holes in a hog's schnoz?

I got my answer about four hours later when the owner showed up with the pig. Sure enough, it had a quarter-sized discoloration on the end of its nose. Obviously, it was a very good pig except for that burned spot.

About ten minutes later, the tattoo dude arrived.

"Holy mackerel!" was all I could say to myself as this fellow came ambling across the parking lot with a briefcase full of tattooing supplies. He stood about six-seven, three hundred pounds, and his entire exposed surface was covered with tattoos.

The pig needed castrating, so I sedated him and quickly removed the testicles. With my job completed, I stepped back and watched as this giant tattooed man began unpacking his arsenal of tattoo gear. He explained that he had built the tattoo gun from a VCR motor and that it was the most powerful one around—just right for a hog's tough nose skin.

His next move made our jaws drop. He pulled off one boot and sock, exposing the top of his foot, on which he had tattooed about twenty thin lines of various shades of reddish-brown. The tattoos looked fresh, still red and irritated on the edges. He then held the foot next to the sedated pig's nose and asked which shade best matched the nose's natural color.

"Dude, did you tattoo those lines on your foot just for this?" I asked incredulously.

"Yep. When I saw that hog on Monday, I realized I would never be able to match the color if I didn't have som'in' to compare it to," he replied.

So there we stood, maybe seven people at varying distances, trying to decide which color line on the man's foot most closely matched the pig's nose.

Can you imagine this giant man holding his foot three feet off the ground next to the nose of a sedated pig. He moves it back and forth so that each line briefly touches the nose for accurate comparison.

After a great deal of debate, we decided on a color, and he went to work.

It took him about fifteen minutes. The result was smashing. You couldn't tell the slightest difference between the color of the normal nose and the tattoo.

The thrilled owner pulled out his wallet and gave the guy forty dollars.

Forty dollars? I charged the owner more than that to sedate the pig and castrate it.

That guy tattooed his own foot and then a pig's nose for forty dollars?

I don't know what I was expecting. I guess I was just going on what I would have charged someone to tattoo my foot and then the nose of a pig.

You can bet it would be somewhere in the six-figure range.

Tall Cow, Fat

The trailer rolled into the parking lot of the clinic, eliciting sighs of awe and amazement from the group of onlookers. Mr. Pep was his name, and he was bringing in his sick cow. The other clients who happened to be at the clinic with me stood with dropped jaws as he pulled across the expanse from the road to the building.

It's not every day you see a cow riding on a flatbed trailer. This was no ordinary flatbed; it must have been five feet off the ground, and it had a cow strapped down on it with those "come along"-type straps that people use to bind round bales—not your ordinary bovine-delivery method.

Ol' Pep had called early that morning to tell me that he had a "real sick" cow that I needed to come out and examine. My reply included phrases such as, "I'm really busy this morning. It will be quite a while before I can get away. It would be better if you could bring her in. I don't want anything to happen to her, so we could get to her quicker if you could load her up." And, "Get her here as quick as you can."

It was now 5:00 p.m., and I had almost completely forgotten he had phoned.

Strapped to that trailer was the skinniest cow I had ever seen. She looked like something from an Ace Reid cartoon. Every rib was visible, and her flanks were so sunken they almost touched in the middle. I was amazed.

"What are you feeding her, Pep?" was all I could think to say as I stood over her.

"I got a giant pile of food for 'em out there," he replied with great conviction.

"Do all of your cows look like this?" was the next logical question.

"No. About half of 'em are big and fat."

I learned early on in my career that the last thing you ever want to do is argue with an opinionated cow raiser about nutrition. So, I treated the cow the best I could, and Pep went merrily on his way.

Three days later, he called me to treat another cow. This time, things around the clinic were quiet, so I drove out to his place on the outskirts of Clarendon. Pep told me that the cow we treated at the clinic was much better, but another one had gone down, and two or three others were in bad shape. What I saw when I arrived amazed me. He must have had a hundred cows grazing in what looked like a junkyard.

As I stood in the middle of Pep's "pasture," I assessed the herd. He was right; some of the cows were big and fat, but others were as poor as any cattle I had seen in my life. My mind raced with every differential diagnosis they had filled my brain with in vet school. I considered disease, poisoning, old cows with bad teeth, and other afflictions with big, Latin-sounding words.

As I pondered the situation with puzzlement and perplexity, it suddenly hit me: all the fat cows were tall, and all the short cows were skinny. My eyes moved from cow to cow . . . tall cow, fat . . . short cow, skinny . . . tall cow, fat . . . short cow, skinny. There was no variance as I scanned the entire herd.

"Pep, where is this pile of food you told me about?"

"Over there behind the barn."

"You mind if I have a look at it?"

"Shoot, no. Come on over."

As we rounded the corner, I found my diagnosis. There, about ten feet behind the barn, was another flatbed that was five feet off the ground. A large group of the short cattle were straining their necks, trying to reach to the "giant pile" of food that the tall cows had eaten back from the edge.

I counseled with Pep for a while about pushing that feed off the trailer so the short cows could get to it. I could tell he thought that was going to be too much work, but he grudgingly agreed that he would do something to remedy the situation.

I drove by Mr. Pep's place about a month later and decided to stop by to see how the short cows were faring. He was nowhere to be found, so I drove on over to the pasture and checked on the cows. Things looked good—tall cow, fat . . . short cow, fat.

You'll never believe how Pep had addressed the problem. There, in the same spot as before, was the flatbed trailer with a pile of food on it. The only difference was that Pep had apparently hired a backhoe to dig a pit into which he could park the trailer. Now the trailer was lower to the ground, and all the cattle could get to the pile.

They just can't teach you stuff like this in vet school.

Pigs at a Football Game

Friday nights in the fall mean only one thing—high school football. All over America, fans flock on cool evenings to cheer for their boys as the "pigskin" is passed, kicked, and handed off. This Friday night was no different, except, perhaps, for the type of pigskin that was involved.

The phone rang about three o'clock. It was a concerned pig owner. It sounded as if one of his prizewinning show hogs had developed a cyst after a recent castration. His voice was filled with the sound of "too many things to do" as he described how hopelessly cluttered his schedule was for the next few days.

"Do you reckon you could meet me at the football game tonight and fix that pig for me?" he asked.

The silence hung as I contemplated the request.

"I figure that the stadium is about halfway between us, and I sure would appreciate it if you could help me out here," he said.

A sarcastic "great" was the first thing to enter my mind in the seconds that passed as I formulated an answer for this request. How was I going to do surgery on a pig, in the dark, at a six-man football game? It was freezing, and besides, I had already made plans with my family for the evening. My mind was telling me this was a dumb idea, but duty called, and I kinda felt sorry for this fellow after hearing the sob story that prefaced his far-fetched request.

It was pitch-black when I arrived at the football field at eight o'clock. Six-man football in West Texas can be very competitive or an absolute blowout. When you have only forty-two kids in the entire high school, it is sometimes hard to even round up six boys who want to play.

The scoreboard read twenty-eight to nothing in the second quarter. The stands were sparsely populated with a few heavily clothed fans who, I could tell, were blowing frost with each exhale. I pulled up to the visiting team's end zone, where under the last set of lights illuminating the field, was the trailer filled with my mission. I was amazed that this guy had parked a trailer in the end zone of a football field and even more amazed that no one had asked him to move it. But at these little football fields, it can be kinda hard to tell where the parking lot ends and the football field begins.

"I figured this was the best light in the county," he said. "If you need some help, just holler. We'll be sitting right over there. Our boy is playing quarterback tonight, and we don't want to miss a play. Oh, by the way, some of our neighbors threw in a few more pigs that just need castrating."

The "great" that had filled my mind earlier now had gone from sarcastic to disgusted.

I gathered all the tools needed for the task at hand and entered the trailer. It didn't take long for the squealing and fighting to get started. I entered the back compartment of the trailer first and determined to tackle the castrations before moving on to the the front compartment. The pigs squealed and rocked the trailer as each injection of sedative went in.

I was done and ready to go on to the critters in the front within ten minutes. As I opened the gate leading deeper into the trailer, I realized that there was just one pig there. He was a monster! Hanging out of his back end was the infected "cord" just begging to be cut off. I sure hated to have to sedate such a large pig on this freezing night simply to snip off a little cord that had become inflamed. I contemplated my options carefully and decided it would be safer for the pig if I just snared his nose and snipped the cord off. It would take just a second and would be painless, almost like ripping off a Band-Aid with a quick jerk instead of pulling it off slowly.

I set about snaring the critter. We bounced off every surface of that trailer as I missed time and time again. That rascal had obviously been snared before and didn't like it one bit. The more I tried and missed, the more determined I became to catch him. The trailer rocked, and the pig screamed. Finally, after what seemed like five minutes and a bath in pig excrement, I caught the monster and secured him to the trailer. It took less than a second to remove the cyst, and I set the pig free. My ears were ringing from five minutes of squeals so loud they rivaled a 747 taking off. My shoulder ached from being pogoed off the walls and stepped on a few times. Nevertheless, the fact that it was finally over quelled my discomfort as I headed for the back gate to make my exit.

As I stepped out into the light of the end zone and brushed myself off, I couldn't help but notice how quiet it was. I was beginning to think that the game was over and everyone had left, when a thunderous cheer met me.

They had stopped the game, and the referee was standing on the five-yard line looking with concerned eyes at me. Both stands were cheering for me, as they evidently had found more entertainment in screaming pigs in a rocking trailer than in the lopsided game. The players were behind the ref, clapping along with the fans.

As I drove home, I couldn't help but think that nowhere but in rural America could you stop a football game for a pig castration.

Meatballs

"Hey, Doc, I got a question for ya. I ate some dog medicine, and I just need to know if it is gonna kill me."

These were the words I was greeted with first thing as I rolled into the parking lot of the clinic at seven o'clock Wednesday morning. And coming from Butchee, those words could do nothing except evoke wonderment and make me laugh.

But he had no humorous expression on his face. In fact, his face was twisted up a bit with worry.

Butchee is a big fella. I don't mean fat or outta-shape-kinda big, either. He's just a big man. He's pushin' fifty and is a hardworking farmer around here. I have known him for twenty years. He has a dog named Gator that makes every mile and every moment with him. Gator is a big yellow Lab that is getting a little old, too.

Butchee's wife had brought Gator into the clinic on Monday, and Dr. Dustin McElwee had dispensed some NSAIDs for ol' Gator to combat the aches and pains that come from being a loyal farm dog for nine years. Dustin told her to put the pill in a piece of cheese or a meatball, and Gator would just eat it up.

Mrs. Butchee got home that Monday evening and was delighted to find that a few of the meatballs she had prepared for Sunday dinner were still in the fridge. Perfect. Dr. Dustin had said meatball, and she just happened to have seven left. It appeared that she now had a vehicle for an entire week's worth of Gator's pain pills.

Mrs. Butchee took one of the meatballs out and poked a pill into it. She was about to take it outside to Gator when the phone rang. It was a call from her mother, who needed immediate help with something. So Mrs. Butchee drove over to Mom's, leaving the one spiked meatball and six normal meatballs sitting on the counter.

A little while later, Butchee arrived home after a hard day's work and saw seven meatballs just begging to be eaten. He slurped them all down and went on about his evening.

When Mrs. Butchee arrived back home, she had forgotten all about the dog pain pills and the meatballs. And since Butchee actually cleaned up the mess, there was nothing to remind her.

"Let me tell you som'in', Doc. Them pain pills you gave Gator work! I ran around the farm yesterday like a little kid. I was jumping over fences, and my back felt better than it has in years. I couldn't figure out why I felt so good. I felt so good yesterday that I just up and challenged Deaver—a twenty-year-old college boy—to an arm-wrestling match at the gin and whipped him.

"The missus forgot all about them pills until this morning. When she remembered Doc Dustin had given them to her, she looked high and low for those meatballs and then asked me if I had seen them. When I told her I ate them all, she just started laughing and asked me if one of them tasted funny. Yeah, I ate that pill," Butchee said. "You reckon that pill gonna have any bad effects on me?"

I could tell this was a trick question. If I told Butchee that the pill wasn't gonna hurt him, he was gonna take the rest of them and forget about ol' Gator. There was too much conviction in his description of how good he had felt all day Tuesday for me to believe that dog would ever get another pill.

I decided to use farmer logic. I raised one eyebrow and replied, "Have you had the urge to hike your leg when you pee? Have you felt like lapping up water with just your tongue? Do you feel like you would rather ride in the bed of the pickup than the cab?"

He kinda got a faraway, thoughtful look on his face and replied, "Nope."

"Well then, I guess you didn't get enough in that one pill, but if you take any more of them, you might start feeling those symptoms." I kept an extremely straight face and left that one, hiked eyebrow hanging.

"Are you kidding with me, Doc? Is that why they are dog pills? You mean to tell me that if I woulda took another one today, I might start acting like a dog? I guess they are *dog* pills. Good thing I talked to you. I felt so good yesterday, I started to take another one. Dang."

I don't know if he believed me or not. He kept looking at me to see if he could read any expression on my face that might indicate if I was joking or serious. I do know that Gator got the rest of the pills. And I do know that every time I see Butchee, he wants to know if I was kidding with him or telling the truth.

Mentors and colleagues are what makes fixing animals a brotherhood. I am passing on what people took the time to teach me every day that I live. It is a sweet tradition that has saved animal after animal over the years. It reminds me of how cowboys have passed on an unwritten code of life and practice since the early days of America. Veterinarians have a network of communication that amazes me even today. On any given week I talk to twenty or so veterinarians that are either asking me questions about a case, or I am asking them. We work behind the scenes to figure out how to make animals happy, and most people never know it even happens. When I look back on my career I find these conversations precious. When they were happening, I considered them to be essential, and now that I have lived through them, I find them to be charming and bonding.

—— *Three* ——

Mentors, Colleagues, and Peers

It is hard to wrap my brain around how much the last twenty-five years of being a veterinarian has effected me. I have learned that no one is an island, even if you live in the middle of nowhere. Some of my richest memories are of other veterinarians that have come through my life. I have mentored some and been mentored by others, but we are all a lot better because we shared our time and experiences.

Dustin McElwee, Kacey Tweeten, and Michelle Dockter came into my life when my practice had expanded way past the abilities of two veterinarians. The effects of being too busy for too long were taking their toll on us, so I hired all three vets all at the same time in 2007. This turned out to be the best thing I ever did.

At first, having three new graduates in the office was a cluster. New graduates don't know how to do much more than study and take tests. I was constantly bombarded with their questions and had to keep my eye on them all the time to make sure they didn't get in over their heads.

But Dustin, Kacey, and Michelle became the backbone of our clinic. They are wonderful veterinarians and even better people. They take care of me and their hard work has allowed me the time to do other things beside working eighty hours per week.

We have six or seven veterinarians on staff now. I think someday we will have even more. Each and every one of them make being a veterinarian in Lamesa, Texas, wonderful.

Teamwork

The result of working with the same people day after day is that a spirit of teamwork develops. We've created that at Brock Veterinary Clinic and it helps us ride the highs and lows of being together all the time.

It's hard to believe that nearly a year has passed since Dr. Zach Smith and his family arrived in Lamesa. They have been a great addition to the practice and have delivered many new ideas and smiles to the area. We are blessed to have them.

I think I remember the moment that Dr. Smith and I crystalized our team bond. It was a blistering-hot day in August—one in a seemingly endless string of blistering summer days. Nothing unusual about having a few goats at the clinic that time of year. Most of the prospective show goats are having cosmetic dehorns done to get ready for the upcoming show season. The surgery rivals a dentist standing on your head to remove a wisdom tooth for being the most gruesome procedure known to man.

This technique requires heavy sedation.

As is often the case, we were working on four goats for which the owners had paid "way too much" money. The people had driven from about a hundred miles away just to have the cosmetic dehorn performed. They dropped off the goats and left to run a few errands.

It was a typical day at the clinic, with a few people standing around either waiting their turns or just watching and asking questions. We had finished the first goat and it was recovering. Recovery usually consists of a gradual wearing off of the heavy sedative, and a slow progression from lying on its side, to lying on its stomach, to standing, to walking with a wobble, to walking, to normal. The whole recovery process usually takes about two or three hours.

I was just about to fill the syringe in my left hand with the medicine in my right hand when I caught a glimpse of movement in my peripheral vision. It must be instinctive in veterinarians, because Dr. Smith noticed the movement at about the same moment.

Having a veterinary clinic right off one of the busiest streets in town has attuned me to the importance of restraining our patients. It only took one two-thousand-pound bull charging down Dallas Avenue while Wyndell Culp rode behind him on horseback, swinging a rope, to drive this point home.

The series of events that followed the blip in my peripheral vision seemed to proceed in slow motion for me. I watched the events unfold almost as if they were happening to someone else, and I was merely a spectator. The critter made a soft goat sound and then sprang to its feet. Remember, the "spring to the feet and walk normal" part is not supposed to occur for a couple of hours and should be preceded by some wobbly walking. The open garage door beckoned Mr. Goat with the promising light of freedom and reminded Dr. Smith and me that beyond it were no fences.

It may not come as a surprise to you that most animals can outrun a person. It also may not surprise you to learn that the human body can do some pretty amazing things when the adrenal glands kick in. I am not certain, but I think it is quite possible that the adrenal glands of the good doctors Smith and Brock deployed completely as that high-dollar goat from a hundred miles away rounded the corner and headed for the open parking lot.

It was truly a team effort from that moment on. We kept up well; Zach on the goat's left side and me on its right. It was one of those moments when I was running so fast that my body was incapable of doing anything else. I believe Dr. Smith was feeling the same, because for about a hundred yards, we simply ran along beside Mr. Goat. I looked at the vial and syringe in my hand and thought, *Throw them down, Bo! Come on, just throw them down.* But I couldn't. I just kept running, looking at the goat with one eye and thinking, *Why can't I throw down this syringe?*

As we caught sight of a trailer approaching at about twelve o'clock, without any form of communication whatsoever, Dr. Smith and I formulated the exact same plan. We would just stay on either side of the goat, and when he reached the trailer, he'd just have to stop.

We got to the trailer. The goat stopped.

Dr. Smith continued along the left side of the trailer, and I continued along the right. We met on the other end of the trailer, each of us expecting the other was still with the goat. It only lasted a second, because the goat was now off again.

Once again, we were off in a flash as the goat was headed for the street. I cannot speak for Zach's thoughts, but I can tell you every one of mine with painstaking detail—first and foremost, change the direction of the goat.

I accelerated with a burst of speed that surprised me—and the goat—but Dr. Smith saw it coming and had slowed just enough to let the goat turn away from me and away from the road dangers ahead. Now the goat headed for the neighboring gas station and I had a shot at actually nabbing the thing. But how was I going to grab a goat with my hands full? Not only that, but was I going to be able to do a diving Pete Rose slide with my hands outstretched? I hadn't done that since the seventh grade.

I knew it was going to take this type of a Hail Mary because we just could not gain any ground on the goat. We would speed up, and he would too. We would slow down, and he would too. No matter how fast we went, he was going to stay just far enough ahead that we couldn't touch him. Just for a second, I tried running while being bent forward at the waist, thinking that this might close the elusive inches that separated us. I felt myself beginning to dive in for the catch and was wondering how I was going to break my fall with the vial of medicine and syringe in my hands. I was keenly aware at this moment why most professional athletes are long retired by my age.

While I tried to coordinate my offensive capture, Dr. Smith went horizontal. There was a brief, fleeting moment when I saw him fly like Superman over what seemed like twenty yards. His left arm grabbed the back leg of the goat, and I was flooded with relief for the first time in what seemed like a day.

One problem remained. I still had to stop myself, but I had not fully recovered from having my center of gravity too far forward. I executed the eleven basic ballet movements as my feet and legs struggled desperately to get back under my torso. Anyone looking at me during this most ungraceful moment must have been thinking, *Why in the world doesn't he throw down that bottle?*

After a few minutes of high-fiving and hard breathing, it became apparent that we were now officially a team. The goat went home, and the owners never even knew anything happened.

I sat in the coolness of the clinic, holding a bottle of medicine and a syringe, and wondering where my youth had gone.

Dr. Deyhle

The day ended late, and I was just about at the end of my endurance when it occurred to me that I hadn't talked to Dr. Deyhle in quite a while. He had been my mentor and took the risk of hiring me straight out of veterinary school. He is in his mid-eighties now, and has been retired about ten years, but he still is more quick-witted than most forty-year-olds.

I had received news a few days earlier that our clinic had earned a practitioner award, and I wanted to give him a call and thank him for helping me get off to a good start all those years ago. To this day, I credit him for instilling an attitude and ethic in me that have persisted.

I was in the middle of thanking him for all he did for me when he interrupted me. After saying he was proud of me and all the accomplishments I've been blessed with in Lamesa, he proceeded to remind me of the first dog I spayed when I joined his practice. I could feel my cheeks turning red as he began to recall the details.

The dog was a big, fat Labrador retriever owned by a decrepit old man who told me it had been given to him by his deceased wife. He said the dog meant more to him than anything in the world.

To make matters worse, the dog was in heat. If you are not a seasoned dog spayer, you may not know that there is nothing worse than a big, fat dog in heat. The fat makes everything slick, and the blood vessels are huge and hard to ligate because of the massive amount of encasing tissue.

I had spayed no more than ten dogs in my vet-school career, and none could have prepared me for this one. I was so dumb I didn't even know to be afraid until I cut that gal open.

Nothing looked like it had in school. Everything was coated with a thick layer of fat, and I could barely identify any of the anatomy. One of the key elements of a spay surgery is tying off all the blood vessels that feed the ovaries and uterus. If you don't do that correctly, the dog could bleed to death. But you have to find the vessels before you can tie them off.

I finally found the artery going to the left ovary and began tying it. All seemed to be going great until I cut the ovary away and blood squirted all over the room. I could feel my first real case of surgical panic coming on.

"Dr. Deyhle! Dr. Deyhle! You gotta come quick!"

All I could think about was breaking the news to this old fella that his most important possession had passed away.

Where was Dr. Deyhle!

I called out again and again, with no response. I began to spiral into a frenzy. If something didn't happen pretty quickly, this critter was going cold. I finally took off at a dead run throughout the clinic, looking for him.

Not in his office. Not in the large-animal clinic. Not in the waiting room. Not with the secretaries. *Where in the world could he be?*

The secretary quickly pointed to the bathroom. The look on my face must have told her that words were wasted.

Can you imagine: Just out of school, you're spaying your first dog for a man who has nothing else to live for. You have dropped the stump, and the only person who can save you is . . . well, indisposed.

Not wanting to break sterility, I began banging on the bathroom door with my elbow, hollering so loud and so fast I didn't even understand my own words.

Dr. Deyhle must have picked up on the urgency. He emerged from the bathroom with his shirt untucked and his pants undone. I will never forget the look on his face—somewhere between panic and embarrassment—as he held up his pants with one hand and fumbled with the bathroom doorknob with the other. He short-stepped down the hall, still holding up his pants.

The tech quickly gloved him, and he went to work fixing everything I'd done wrong. In no time, the bleeding was stopped, and he finished spaying the dog. In fact, he did the entire surgery with his legs apart to keep his pants from dropping. We couldn't find one volunteer to button and zip them while he worked.

"You've come a long way since those days, Bo, but I just want you to know that you will always be a snotty-nosed, novice veterinarian to me. That is how you were when I met you, and you had barely passed that stage by the time you left."

I just love that man.

Dr. Tweeten Saves the Day

It is quite an adjustment from veterinary school to Lamesa, Texas. It was an especially unique adjustment for Dr. Kacey Tweeten, who grew up in North Dakota, graduated from Iowa State University, and wound up in West Texas.

This particular Friday night in West Texas was like all other fall Fridays: football night. We West Texans watch six-man football in the middle of a cotton field, eat hamburgers, and stand around and talk. That's how we kick off our weekends.

Steven, the father of one of the cheerleaders, and I were in charge of cooking hamburgers for the home team. The nights were getting chilly, bringing welcome relief from the heat, and especially from flies and mosquitoes.

I like to take pictures of the football game, so I headed for the sidelines after cooking. Steven, on the other hand, likes to visit. So, he finished cooking and stood next to the grill, talking about show pigs and farming with anyone who wandered by.

Shortly thereafter, Dr. Tweeten called to inform me that a sick horse was on its way to the clinic. I had a couple of things to do at home, so I left the game to take care of them before I had to spend the rest of the evening doing colic surgery.

I had been home only a minute when Kerri called to say that Steven needed some help. I couldn't imagine what it might be. The game was over and the burgers were long gone.

"A bug flew into his ear, and we can't get it out. Will you meet him at the clinic and see if you can get it out?" Kerri asked.

A bug? It was forty-nine degrees outside. How could a bug fly into someone's ear at that temperature?

"What kind of bug?" I asked, feeling a chuckle coming on.

"A moth. You know, one of those Miller moth things," Kerri replied, as a car door slammed in the background.

"I am at home, but Dr. Tweeten is up there. I'll be there in a bit. She can get it out," I replied as the chuckle became a giggle.

As I finished my jobs around the house, I found myself laughing aloud. What were the chances of a sizeable moth flying into someone's ear? It would really have to tuck its body in to fit. I kept picturing the insect zooming in from fifty feet in the air, its wings pressed in to its sides like an Olympic diver's arms. Of all the thousands of square feet at that football game, what were the odds that the moth would insert itself into an earhole and not even hit the rim?

I called the clinic on my way in to see what was happening. Dr. Tweeten answered on the first ring. She seemed to be stifling a laugh.

"Did you get the bug out of Steven's ear?" I asked without preamble, trying to keep from laughing.

"Yep, it was killing him. Seems it wouldn't quit flapping its wings, and the noise and vibration were driving him nuts. It was so deep you couldn't even see it without the otoscope. He was holding his head sideways and pushing on his tragus (that little nub on the front part of your ear) to keep the thing from banging against his eardrum. I finally got it out. It was bigger than a nickel! I let it go, but he ran and caught it and then stomped it. How in the world could a bug bigger than a nickel dive-bomb an earhole? It was a perfect fit," she said.

By then I was laughing so hard I could barely drive, and Dr. Tweeten was laughing so hard she could barely finish the story.

I am not sure why it's so funny to me, but it's hilarious. I am still cracking up as I write this. I guess it is just the fact that a nickel-sized bug could isolate and insert itself into an earhole on a forty-nine-degree night and get in so deep that it required a veterinarian to remove it.

Small-town veterinarians fill a niche that includes more than just putting animals back together.

Boy and a Hoe

It seems like every plant in West Texas has a thorn, and every animal some kind of sting. Dry, dusty environments require toughness to survive. I have spent my entire life here, so I guess I just assumed that every place was just like that.

Not so. People come here from faraway places, and when they do, they remind me that the whole world is much different than West Texas.

Dr. Emily is our new intern. She is a feisty, hardworking country girl who moved to West Texas from the Central Valley of California. This little gal works like a sled dog and seemed to fear nothing, but she had never seen a rattlesnake or treated the effects of a venomous snakebite on the head of a horse.

About a week into her internship, she did. The horse came in looking like they all do: head so swollen it could barely breathe, eyes running with goo, and skin splitting. It looked miserable.

She spent a long time looking at this poor critter and commenting on how awful it must be to get bitten by one of those slithering varmints. I could see her brain calculating what one of those bites would do to a hundred-pound intern if it could do that much damage to a twelve-hundred-pound horse. She nursed that horse through the incident and made many comments about how sorry she felt for it. I could tell she was gaining a healthy respect for, as well as a major fear of, the western diamondback.

A few weeks passed, but the memory of that horse and the dreaded snake did not dim much for Dr. Emily. Her conversations with clients and other people at the clinic often veered toward identification, daytime hiding places, and the normal habitat of rattlesnakes and diamondbacks. One client mentioned that many snakes had ceased rattling when startled. His theory was simple survival of the fittest: all the ones that rattled got their heads cut off with a hoe by some cowboy or farmer, and so they had evolved away from the rattle.

This concept worried her even more. How was one to be alerted to one of these killer beasts if it just sat silent, camouflaged, and motionless? This seemed to raise her awareness of the environment even more.

One warm July morning, as I walked from one barn to another at the clinic, I heard a faint noise in the distance. The noise was obviously a person, and obviously, that person was in distress. I wasn't sure if the commotion was getting closer to me or if the distress was just getting louder.

Before I could sort out the exact source, I saw the problem. It was Dr. Emily. She was screaming over and over: "I need a boy and a hoe! I need a boy and a hoe!"

I arrived at the stall she was pointing toward while she danced about and informed me that a giant rattler was in the stall with a horse. Her eyebrows had relocated up at her hairline, and her lips were tight with terror as she continued to call for a hoe before her patient acquired a swollen head.

I saw one of the guys look into the stall at the snake and immediately knew there was no giant rattler in there. He just kind of smiled and walked into the stall without the much-needed hoe. Dr. Emily's eyes got even wider as he started herding the bull snake back out into the pasture.

"What are you doing?" she screeched. "That thing could make your head swell up and cause all the skin to break and your nose holes to collapse! You just gonna run it off? It will come back!"

The fellow just kinda giggled and assured Emily that it was just a rowdy bull snake. They don't hurt anything, so we don't kill 'em.

"What do you mean they don't hurt anything? I about prolapsed trying to get away from it! That thing was six feet long and hissing, and you're just gonna let it go? It could have given that horse, and *me*, heart failure. *I hate snakes!*"

Dr. Box

Dr. Ronald Box is a brilliant veterinarian from Pecos, Texas. Ranchers and other veterinarians consider him the go-to doctor for difficult cases in West Texas and New Mexico.

Dr. Box is also a great storyteller. He recently told me of an incident that typifies certain days in the life of a rural veterinarian.

He had pulled up to the locked gate leading into a large, West Texas ranch. The owner was to meet him there, and they were to go down to the pens together to palpate the cows and work the calves.

The owner, a highly successful and passionate rancher who had accumulated a fortune, called on Dr. Box to keep the animals healthy at all of his properties.

The owner soon arrived and, after exchanging a few greetings through the rolled-down window of his pickup truck, told Dr. Box to go ahead and open the gate so they could move down to the pens.

Dr. Box, who had not visited this newly purchased ranch before, noticed that someone had shot a hole through the middle of the lock, but it was still holding. He asked for a key, but the owner shouted back that he didn't even know the gate had a lock.

After the doctor spent several minutes trying to jimmy the lock open, the ranch owner grew tired of waiting and stepped out to help. They each pulled a few tools from their trucks and managed to work the lock mechanism to the point that it finally slid open. But it wouldn't swing open quite far enough for them to get the end of the chain loose. That prompted another trip to the toolboxes.

Here stood one man with an excellent college education, and another who'd earned millions in business, but the two of them had now spent more than thirty minutes simply trying to get into the ranch so they could start working. Every attempt was fruitless.

It was beginning to look as though they would have to chop down the gatepost.

They were so absorbed in the task that they hadn't noticed a cowboy ride up on his horse. He had come from the working pens inside to find out why the two were taking so long at the gate. They finally took notice of the cowboy when he spoke.

"The gate opens on the other side," he said, then quietly turned around and rode back to the pens.

Neither Dr. Box nor the rancher had taken the time to observe that they were working on the side of the gate with the hinges. They'd just seen the chain with the lock on it and busied themselves at trying to open it.

"A bit humbling" was how Dr. Box described the experience to me.

It's no wonder cowboys and ranch hands think that veterinarians and rich landowners can be a bit tiresome at times.

Dr. Beaver

Hands are often a reflection of one's life. The cracks, calluses, and bit-off nails tell the story of how a day is spent.

I was sitting through the second hour of a board of directors meeting for the Texas Veterinary Medical Association, paying more attention to my hands than to the topic of the moment. Winter always seems to make them uglier than usual. The knuckles get deep, there are bleeding cracks, and the skin seems to get so dry it's probably a fire hazard.

I was looking at the skin on the top of my left hand, and wondering if it was about to dry up and fall off, when the veterinarian sitting to my left pulled out some lotion. She must have seen my hands and been reminded of what truly ugly hands look like.

"Would you mind if I had a little of that?" I asked like a twelve-year-old asking for some lemonade.

"You don't want any of this; it smells too feminine," she replied with an air of confidence that made me feel as if she was an expert dermatologist. "I've got a different kind in my purse that would work better on those hands."

After digging around for a bit, she pulled out a tube that had

"Shea" written on it in bold letters. I was encouraged. I proceeded to squeeze a generous portion into one hand and began to rub it in.

This stuff was amazing, but it never seemed to absorb; it just kinda spread out. After twenty minutes of vigorous rubbing that very well could have been misconstrued as a nervous disorder, my hands were still so slick I could barely pick up my pen.

I tried to wipe some onto the tablecloth, but it didn't want to transfer. In fact, I think I made it angry enough to multiply. The only noticeable change was the blinding sheen that began to form, as if I were buffing it. I could almost see my own reflection.

My next thought was to blow them dry. Like a pitcher on the mound in October, I began the procedure, but it was fruitless. I finally just gave up.

I wasn't sure what this stuff was, but judging by its staying power, I was pretty sure it'd last me the rest of the winter.

As the meeting crept into the third hour, I decided to sneak back to the coffee urn for a warm-up, when I heard someone whisper my name.

To my surprise, the president of the American Veterinary Medical Association (AVMA) was just a few feet away. I couldn't believe she knew my name. In fact, I was a bit flabbergasted that someone with her credentials and standing would know a small-town veterinarian from West Texas.

She smiled and extended her hand while I instinctively reached out to greet her. The tighter she gripped my hand, the harder it was to hold on to. It just sort of slid away.

She glanced down to see what she had just grabbed, revealing a polished hand covered in what could have been Crisco. Less than five seconds later, with my cheeks piping hot, I retreated to the coffee table.

I took a little extra time fixing my drink, wondering exactly what she must be thinking. I had some ideas, but I didn't like any of them.

I decided it might be better to just walk out the back door rather than face her again. As I headed to the washroom, I looked over in time to see her rubbing her hand on her tablecloth.

Neither soap nor water was any match for this stuff. Water beaded off my hands as it would a freshly waxed car. I spent the rest of the day trying to avoid anyone I knew and dodging situations where I might need to shake someone's hand so I could contain the slickest substance known to man.

It occurred to me that Shea stuff would make good bearing grease. Or maybe Olympic bobsled teams could trim a few seconds off their time if they used it on their runners.

At least that AVMA president would never forget me. In fact, she might still have a very shiny, slippery, but exceptionally well moisturized right hand.

Blodgett

The clock read 6:00 as Dr. Glenn Blodgett settled into his butt-hungry easy chair to absorb the mindless callings of a Friday-evening football game on ESPN. His day started early at the ranch, and four-thirty in the morning felt like it had been ages ago. How wonderful an evening of rest sounded after the stress of running a veterinary clinic for a full week.

The clock read six thirty when his phone rang. Seemed a horse was colicking, and the intern was concerned by how fast it had come on and how severe the symptoms were. This was a valuable critter, and ol' Doc figured he should go back to the clinic and put his eyes on it. Shouldn't take but a few minutes, and then the easy chair would welcome him back for the second half of the game.

Great. The colic wasn't responding to medication, and surgery might be needed. Lamesa was a two-hour drive, but it was looking like this horse was gonna need to make the trip. Let's see, Blodgett considered, *it's 7:00 p.m. It'll be about nine by the time we get there. About an hour and a half for surgery, another two hours home: I should be tucked comfortably in bed by a little past midnight.*

The horse made the trip well and seemed to be almost normal. What then? Dr. Blodgett thought that maybe he should hang out in Lamesa awhile to see if anything changed. *Let's see,* he thought, *what does tomorrow hold? Oh yeah, there's an important veterinarian coming to the ranch to interview for a job. She won't be there until nine or ten. If I stay for an hour or so more to watch, I should still get enough sleep to be reasonably entertaining and hospitable.*

Why do things have to be so complicated? There was an hour of improvement and then another round of pain. Not the kind of pain that sent the horse into surgery; just enough to keep the doc from going home.

The clock on the wall of the operating room read 4:30 a.m. when we finally made the incision to start the surgery. The next clock assessment occurred at 7:00 a.m. as the truck pulled out, headed back to Guthrie. Dr. Blodgett would get back in time to take a quick shower and welcome the prospective doctor.

His energy level was surprisingly high all day. When the clock struck 3:00 p.m. on Saturday, the good Dr. Blodgett and his applicant were headed for a gathering in a town an hour away. If everything went as planned, he would be in bed by 9:00 p.m., with a mere forty-two or so hours of sleep deprivation.

Of course, the gathering lasted a bit longer than it was supposed to. The normally happy-go-lucky Dr. Blodgett had entered the "hazy zone," which includes moments of raucous laughter followed by moments of blurred understanding and silliness.

The clock on the dashboard read 10:00 p.m. as they left for the one-hour journey home. No more conversation was available to be squeezed from the exhausted neurons in the cerebrum of Dr. Blodgett. A word now and then to pierce the silence was all that he could muster.

Finally, the sound of the passenger door closing as the visiting doctor headed for the bunkhouse. All that was left to do was conquer two gates and a garage door, and the good Dr. Blodgett would dissolve into bed.

The first gate required manual opening and closing. Easy enough: put the truck in park, open the gate, drive through, park again, close it, on to the next one. The second gate was even better: just drive up, and the motion detector would sense the approaching vehicle and open itself. The clock read 11:15 p.m. Saturday as Dr. Blodgett approached the last gate on a now-forty-three-hour journey to the bed that called his name.

As luck would have it, the dang thing wouldn't open with just the normal motion detection. He put the truck in park, opened the door . . . no wait, the gate was opening.

The clock read 11:45 when Dr. Blodgett saw it next. The extent of his awakeness had ended at 11:15 exactly. He fell soundly asleep behind the wheel of the red Ford pickup, which was still running, as the gate opened and closed. . . . He had hit the end.

A mere one hundred yards from his house, the forty-four-hour journey ended. He had spent every ounce of gas in his awake tank, and could no longer hold his heavy eyes open. Thirty minutes of sleep gave him just enough juice to get to the gate, open it again, and dive into that bed.

What a life we veterinarians have. Absolutely amazing.

Dr. Bill

Dr. Bill is a good friend of mine. He is seventy years old and still practices at a pace that most thirty-year-olds would envy. I check in with him from time to time just to get a reminder of what I need to do to be like him when I grow up. He is a credit to the veterinary profession and an inspiration to me.

A few days ago, we were talking about a horse he was sending to us for surgery, and I mentioned something about prices. I asked him how he went about knowing when it was time to raise prices and how he kept people from having a fit when he did. He proceeded to tell me the story of the cowboy and the dead cows.

A few years back, a couple of old cowboys came into the clinic wanting Dr. Bill to come out to the ranch and post-mortem a couple of dead cows. The cowboys believed that the cattle had gotten into some oil from local oil-field work, and they wanted Bill to come out, take some samples to send off, and confirm their suspicions. Bill was agreeable. He assured them that he would come out and post the cows within the hour.

As they were heading out the door, one cowboy asked how much it cost to cut up a dead cow. Bill replied that it was $300. Seems the cows had been dead for an entire day, and the temperature had been over a hundred degrees. Bill wasn't keen to cut into those cows.

"What? You mean to tell me you gonna charge us almost as much as that cow is worth just to cut her up after she dead? Doc, you're getting to be like them city doctors. That is way too much money to cut up som'in' dead. Why don't you just give me those little sample baggies, and me and Buddy, here, will get them ourselves. What do we got to get? I'm telling you what, you veterinaries are just gettin' outta control. Last time we had you out to cut up a dead cow, it was just a hundred bucks [That was 1976, Dr. Bill amended]. That is reeediculous."

Bill just smiled and replied, "Sure thing. Here are the baggies, and all you have to do is cut open the cow's paunch and put some of the stuff inside of it in this baggy. Then cut into the abdomen, get a foot of small bowel, and put it in this bigger baggy. When you get it, bring it back here, and we will send it off."

A couple of hours later, they showed up at Dr. Bill's. Neither of them looked too happy, and there was a distinct dead-for-too-long-in-the-sun odor coming off them. Their shirts, which had originally been a light-blue color, were now an off-green color with a stiff, starched texture from the dried goo that had erupted from that bloated creature when they punctured it with their knives to retrieve some paunch juice. Their cowboy hats looked as if someone had been sprayed with that bumpy popcorn-ceiling stuff, except that the bumpy stuff was green and smelled like carcass. Their eyes were watering still, and one of them was explaining how he had thrown up three times while driving to the clinic.

"We decided we wanted you to come do it! We musta done som'in' wrong. That thing blew up like a bomb when we stuck a knife in it. It kept spewing for ten minutes, and every time we would run around to the other side, the wind would change direction, and we would get covered some more. I guess three hundred dollars ain't so bad, considering how nasty a person got to get!"

"How much? No, you musta misunderstood me. I said three-fifty!" Dr. Bill smiled and raised one eyebrow.

"That is how you raise prices, Bo. Been doing it like that for forty-five years. No one complains but one time, and then they are glad to pay you!"

Salute to Clifford

It has been almost twenty years since it all began. And I have to thank a skinny surgeon who grew up just north of the Mexico border for showing me the way. It is an amazing story when I look back on it. I never even dreamed it would turn out this way.

Well, that's not entirely true. I dreamed of it. From as far back as I can remember, I wanted to be a horse surgeon. But it's one of those things that's a bit like that water-looking mirage on the road ahead of you on a hot day—it is always ahead of you and you can never catch it. But Dr. Cliff Honnas held that water-looking stuff still long enough that I could actually grab a hold of it.

When I was a fourth-year student at Texas A&M, I was accepted into a surgical internship, but I didn't take it because it only paid

$14,000 a year. At the time, I had a baby girl and could not figure out any way to take care of a child on that meager salary even though it was my chance to learn surgical practice.

You don't learn to be a horse surgeon in veterinary school. If you want to do that, you have to go on and do an internship and a residency in that discipline. No one leaves the curriculum at a veterinary school after four years capable of or qualified to do advanced equine surgery. Turning down that internship, I told myself I would not let go of my dream to practice equine surgery, no matter what. Even if it took thirty years, I was going to be a surgeon and fix horses.

Well, let me tell you, it is terribly hard to get a board-certified horse surgeon to teach a common veterinarian like me how to do these tough surgeries. And I don't blame them. They endured four years of working day and night at poverty-level pay in order to learn their craft, and they really take offense to some country vet trying to do what they sacrificed so much to accomplish.

But good ol' Cliff Honnas always answered the phone. He always took a little time to tell me how to do a surgery when there was no book to explain it or no experience of my own to draw on. Cliff's generosity toward me has saved a huge number of horses in West Texas.

Dr. Honnas began teaching at the Texas A&M veterinary school about the time I left. I'd heard of him, but never officially met him. As I was facing a particularly tough surgery in 1994—and had no clue who I could turn to for guidance—the A&M student working at the clinic suggested I call Cliff Honnas. Well, I did, and we have been friends from that day forward.

Cliff has come to Lamesa a few times now to show me how to execute difficult procedures. I'd offer to cover his travel and give him a modest surgical fee, and he seemed perfectly happy with that. He has always been available to talk me through a new procedure and, as time has passed, there have been fewer and fewer procedures that I hadn't done or didn't know how to do. But we have remained friends.

I never would have been even close to being able to do the things I can do now without his guidance through those early years of uncertainty and doubt. And I really don't think he will ever have any idea how many horses have lived or returned to happiness because of the things he taught me.

Pedro finds his way into my ode to Cliff Honnas because he also figures prominently in my horse-fixin' history. He started using me as a veterinarian long before I knew what I was doing as an equine surgeon.

This fella had confidence in me as a horse doctor and brought in his racehorses at least once a week. We had worked together to keep his horses running fast for a couple of years when one of them came in with a bone chip in its left knee. It needed arthroscopic surgery. At the time, I did not do arthroscopic surgery.

One of my classmates, John Vandermeer, had sent me a few arthroscopes. He had extra arthroscopes on hand because his father had been the team doc for the Dallas Cowboys, and he knew I had a passion for learning to fix horses. But all he sent were the scopes. I had no light source, no fluid pump, no camera or screen, no surgery table, no money to get those things, and worst of all . . . I didn't know how to do the surgery!

Pedro saw the radiograph and told me he would leave the horse for me to remove the chip. I explained that I didn't have the equipment to do it or the money it would take to buy it.

He couldn't believe it. I guess he assumed every vet knew how to do that stuff. He asked how much it would cost to get the stuff I needed to perform the surgery. I told him the bare minimum for used equipment would be a couple thousand dollars. He didn't even blink as he told me he was gonna leave his horse and pay me $2,000 for the surgery and that I should use it to buy what I needed.

Great! What was I going to do now? Just having an airplane doesn't make one a pilot. I had a horse and the desire, placed an order for all the equipment I needed, but no knowledge.

I immediately thought of Cliff. By then, we had become friends, and my only hope was that he would offer some instruction and some luck.

Cliff answered my call on the first ring. I explained my situation, and he immediately gave me a detailed description of what I was about to face and how to get it done, much like he would have done for a resident at the vet school. He described the procedure with a calm and easy attitude, tossing in an occasional joke along the way to lower my blood pressure.

I studied equine knee anatomy deeply for a few days. All of the equipment arrived, and I—along with some of the best supporting cast on earth—went to work. It just happened to be the easiest chip there is to get out of a joint, and we took that rascal out like we had been doing arthroscopy for years.

The serendipity of the situation is not lost on me. How on earth was it possible that I would get a horse with the simplest kind of knee-chip, a generous and trusting owner, a friend who had just the necessary extra equipment lying around, and a mentor like Cliff who was kind enough to share his expert knowledge with me?

That horse went on to win $50,000. Pedro had about 150 horses in his program and was well connected to dozens of trainers who eventually came to us for arthroscopic surgery.

What a blessing. That one surgery resulted in the biggest change that would ever happen in my career. Over the next twenty years, I would log thousands of arthroscopic surgeries. I never had a lesson from anyone but Honnas, and to this day I have never even seen anyone but him perform an arthroscopy.

I'm not entirely sure how many people Dr. Honnas has taught to do arthroscopy, but I'm fairly sure that none of them has performed as many as I have. Because Cliff took the time to answer my phone call, a huge number of horses have gone on to run fast and be happy.

So, here is to Dr. Cliff Honnas. No book by me would be complete without a chapter thanking him for being my friend.

Britt

I try never to judge people by the clothes they wear or the cars they drive, but after eleven years of hot checks and no-pay clients, you start paying attention to subtle clues that might mean you are about to lose some money.

We have been blessed to host many veterinary students over the years, and we consider it a privilege to be a part of their training. This particular summer found us with Britt Conklin. Doctor-to-Be Conklin was a go-getter and always accused me of being the biggest pessimist in the world.

It had been about three straight weeks of working through lunch, and I was really looking forward to eating and resting just a bit before the busy afternoon began. But in walked the driver of an orange Ford Pinto. He was wearing a T-shirt that was so old it had a "run" in it. At his side was a German shepherd that was so skinny you could read a newspaper through him. The only thing on this dog that wasn't totally devoid of normal size was his abdomen. This critter's belly was twice as big around as anything else and kinda jiggled as the dog ambled to the front door of the clinic.

As usual, Britt dove into the case. He filled out a record and took the motley pair into the exam room to work his healing magic. I went to my office and began pouting over another missed lunch.

In a few minutes, Britt was at my office door, listing his findings: heart murmur, congested lungs, ascites, and pallor were just a few of the ailments that came rolling off his highly educated tongue.

"What do you think is wrong, Dr. Brock?" was his final sentence as his eyebrows drifted up his forehead.

"What do I think is wrong?" I replied in a sarcastic tone. "That dog practically has a heartworm crawling out of his nose. Before you do anything to that dog, you make sure the owner of the Pinto understands that the dog is in terrible shape and most likely won't live. Remember, we have to treat heartworm-infested dogs with arsenic to kill the worms, and a dog that sick will have a hard time with the treatment. If the owner decides he wants to treat him, make sure you get a deposit."

"There you go being a pessimist again," bubbled out of his lips as his eyebrows returned to normal position. "You never know what might happen, and you never know how much this guy loves his dog."

He was right and his words made me feel a bit guilty about my judgments. But I couldn't help thinking that if that guy loved his dog so much, why did he let it become a walking skeleton before he brought it in? And as for the money thing, well, treating heartworms is an expensive proposition. It takes very expensive medicine, eight or so weeks of confinement, and serial blood tests to monitor the progress of the patient. Maybe this guy was really a millionaire who just chose to drive an orange Pinto, but I doubted it.

A confident "Let me take care of this" met my ears, and off he went.

A few minutes later, Britt returned with a smile, the news of a deposit, and a signed slip of permission to treat the dog for the now-confirmed case of heartworms. I felt even more guilty.

We routinely run an initial blood test to evaluate whether a dog can tolerate the treatment. As this dog was in terrible shape, we decided to treat the other problems with the liver and kidneys before we subjected the shepherd to the worm-killing dose of arsenic.

Much to my surprise, the next day we found a totally different dog. He could stand up on his own, was wagging his tail, and was eating and drinking like nobody's business. I was beginning to feel some "crow eating" coming on as Britt told me how well the dog had responded to the initial treatment.

All I had to say was, "What kind of odds did you give this guy?"

"Well, yesterday I told him there was a less than 30 percent chance that the dog would live. But when he called this morning, I upped it to 70 percent. He was so excited that he said he would be down in a little while to see."

Just as he had told me, the fellow showed up, and they just went on and on about how well things were going. The Pinto driver shook Britt's hand for a good long time, and departed the clinic with the largest smile I had seen in a while. I could smell the crow cooking as Britt puffed out his chest and returned to the side of his patient.

So far, we had run seventy-five dollars of blood tests, given fifty dollars of medications, run twenty dollars of heartworm tests, put in a catheter, and run forty-five dollars of fluids. Remember, we hadn't even started treating the heartworms yet. I still had my doubts, but Britt spent the entire day walking with a hop in his step.

The next morning, we walked into the kennel together to check out the shepherd's condition. What we found was quite a bit different than it had been the day before: he was so dead that it was shocking. His legs were stiff and poking through the side of the kennel.

"What am I going to do?" shrieked Britt. "This guy thinks his dog is doing great! How could he have died? He was doing great just twelve hours ago. Now he is lying there as if he died two weeks ago! Oh my gosh! This is terrible!"

Britt no longer had a hop in his step as he walked to the office to phone the dog's owner. Doom and gloom were written all over his face as he solemnly told Mr. Pinto the bad news.

For the rest of the summer, Britt was a man of percentages. He couldn't give a vaccination without saying that there was a 30 percent chance the dog may die. By the end of the summer, I took to calling him the eternal pessimist. He informed me that it was a lot easier to tell someone who was expecting his or her dog to die that it had lived than it was to explain how one that was supposed to live had died.

"No kidding," was my reply as I passed the crow pie to him.

When the tenderness of the situation had dulled, I told him that all was not lost: at least he'd gotten a deposit.

"Oh, I was going to tell you about that," Britt said. "Mr. Pinto only had ten dollars on him that day."

Dr. Mark

Dr. Mark Justice explained the events of the previous night with a mixture of regret and relief.

I had seen the horse in question before, and nothing Dr. Mark could have said about it would have surprised me. The critter was huge and stupid. When I say huge, I am not joking. This horse was more than sixteen hands tall (more than sixty-four inches at the shoulder) and must have weighed fourteen hundred pounds. To make matters worse, the horse was spoiled rotten by its owner. It would kick, bite, paw, and bulldoze anyone who made it do anything it wasn't in the mood to do.

Mark had seen the horse the night before, but sent it along to my clinic in Lamesa. And he was calling to apologize.

The owner had called Mark in hysterics. Her horse had run into something in the pasture and sustained an eighteen-inch slash on the front of its left hind leg. The cut was close to a joint and had severed a large blood vessel. Blood was squirting, and muscle tissue was hanging out. The owner was in tears when she met Mark at the truck. She was panicked as she described the situation. Little did he know what he was getting into.

Since it was after hours, Mark asked his new bride to accompany him to see what a typical farm call was like. She followed him over fences and through barns until they came to the critter in question. The owner was right: the cut was deep and in a dangerous place. But she had failed to tell Mark about the look in the horse's eyes. Having worked on thousands of horses, Mark knew when one was a bit snakey. This horse was snakey, and Mark could tell it from across the pasture.

After about fifteen minutes of chasing and sweet-talking, he finally got a halter on the beast. When he stuck the needle into the vein to give the sedative, the horse reared up, pawed, and tried to bite him. He decided that it might be prudent to up the dose a bit. Even with an elephant dose of sedative, the horse was still kicking at him when he tried to clean the wound. So Mark gave more sedative.

Mark was standing in the middle of a pasture with only the lights of a pickup to see what he was doing. A frantic owner and Mark's new bride looked on; each worried about different parties involved. The horse was so tranquilized it could barely stand, but it still lashed out with fly-swatting accuracy. Mark had given an elephant's dose— plus one—and was now trying to administer a local block of lido-caine around the area so he could suture the laceration.

He gently slid the needle holding the numbing agent into an area of the skin that needed to be sutured. To his surprise, the horse just stood there. Maybe the sedative had finally worked! But when he started to inject the medicine, the horse suddenly kicked. The kick hit Dr. Mark's hand and sent the syringe flying twenty yards across the pasture, where it stuck a pecan tree.

So he gave some more sedative.

Funny thing about that sedative—it makes a male horse "drop" his boy part. After the third dose of sedative, not only did the critter finally let him inject the local anesthesia but he had also dropped his boy part. It was hanging down, right in the way of the suturing job, and it was hitting Mark in the head as he tried to sew.

Do you know how hard it is to sew up a horse from a squat while remaining in a position that allows for a quick exit if the need arises? Can you imagine how hard that would be with the added complication of a boy part slapping you in the face? The good doc-tor had finally had enough and reached over to move the offending appendage. This, of course, elicited another vicious kick that sent the needle flying into the darkness of the pasture.

The new bride was getting concerned, the owner was apologizing, and Mark was preparing another dose of sedative.

With both hands bruised, a missing pair of needle holders, a syringe stuck in a pecan tree, a worried wife, and a nagging owner, Mark decided it was time to send this horse to Lamesa, where there was a set of stocks and a way to anesthetize the monster fully.

His voice was filled with regret and relief as he gave me the details. All I could do was laugh as I listened to him apologize for sending me such a mess.

Dr. Smith and the Big Dogs

On my way home from teaching, I noticed the lights were on at the clinic.

I pulled up to see what was going on and found Dr. Zach Smith gathering up equipment to make a farm call. Cows always seem to prolapse in the middle of the night.

Listening to Dr. Smith describe the situation made me think that this might not be your run-of-the-mill prolapse. In fact, it sounded to me like this might be quite an adventure. I asked if I could tag along, and together we loaded up and headed out to rebuild a cow.

The owner of the cow was gone for a few days, and he had left his wife in charge of the herd. As usual, trouble always shows up at the most unwanted times. According to the frantic wife's description, the cow was either "turning inside out" or "giving birth to an elephant, trunk-first."

I guess that would be a good description of a prolapse if you had never seen one before. This woman was not into cows. She was frustrated to have to watch them at all, much less have to chase them into a corral and call out the vet.

We arrived in the middle of nowhere to find the woman sitting inside her pickup with the lights shining into a run-down thirty-by-thirty pen. "Dark" did not do justice to how pitch-black it was. He didn't say anything, but I knew that Dr. Smith and I were thinking the same thing: *How in the world are we going to do this?*

In all my years of making farm calls, I have learned to look around before getting out of the truck. Most farms have dogs, and most of these dogs don't like vets and especially don't like strangers in the cow pens.

I noticed them about the time Dr. Smith said, "Have a look at the size of them dogs!"

There they were—two big Rottweilers and a weenie dog. They didn't really bark; they just stood by the door of the truck and made throaty growls.

The woman got out of her truck and came to the window of ours. She was trying to describe the situation with the cow when Dr. Smith interrupted.

"What about the dogs?"

"They wouldn't bite a biscuit," was her reply, as the pack of them stood next to the window and growled. I wasn't worried about a biscuit. It was veterinarians that concerned me.

She managed to coax us out of the pickup and over to the pens. Dr. Smith did the talking, and I pulled up the rear, watching the dogs. The entire herd—one giant bull and three cows—was in the pen. The cow with the prolapse was one of the thinnest animals I had ever seen. Not only that, but she was crippled. So here she stood, four hundred pounds underweight, crippled in one back leg, and prolapsed. What a specimen.

There was no way to restrain the cow. The pen was just a thirty-by-thirty square with a tin roof over one corner.

Dr. Smith pulled me aside and asked, "How in the world are we gonna do anything for that cow if we can't catch her?"

"I don't know. Let's just go in and see what happens. Anything would be better than standing out here with these dogs growling at us," I said as we climbed over the fence.

The bull was not a bit happy about intruders. He stood in the corner and pawed the ground. The other two cows started running in circles around the pen. This excited the dogs, and they came through the fence. Now we were in the center of the pen trying to get near the skinny, prolapsed cow, with two wild cows circling, a mad bull, a pair of worked-up Rottweilers, and a weenie dog.

We approached the afflicted cow and began sizing up what we might do. As I got closer, I noticed that she didn't move at all. In fact, I could just walk up and touch her. I figured that she would have a hard time kicking with one bad back leg, so I just went to work trying to poke the prolapse back in. She just stood there. Dr. Smith tried to keep the bull and wild cows off me as I struggled to put things back together—like shoving a marshmallow into a piggy bank.

With all the straining and sweating, I had forgotten about the dogs. Suddenly, I heard deep growls. Before I could even react, the dogs grabbed ahold. They bit down for all they were worth. I panicked, but not because they were biting me; it wasn't me they had sunk their teeth into, it was the cow. One Rottweiler had the tail, one had a back foot, and the weenie dog was running in between her legs, barking and jumping. I was afraid to kick them off the cow because they might just turn on me. The cow started running, but I couldn't quit. The marshmallow was just about back in the piggy bank. I gave a mighty lunge forward just as Dr. Smith started hollering at the dogs. The prolapse popped back in, and the dogs scattered.

The woman was very impressed. I guess she thought we did stuff like that every day. You can bet her husband got an earful when he got home. I doubt he'll ever be permitted to leave town again.

Dr. Dockter

Have you ever wondered why the word used to describe an individual under medical care is also used to describe someone with forbearance and endurance? Do you think that's a coincidence? Well, I have been practicing veterinary medicine for nearly twenty years, and I can tell you it's no coincidence.

Are you a patient person? I'm not. In fact, when Dr. Michelle Dockter recently told me about her experience at a supermarket, it prompted some self-evaluation in me. Here's what happened.

She was in a hurry, as we often are, and the checkout lines were long. She sized them up—looking at the volume of items in people's carts—and finally settled on a line in which the customers had just a few items per person.

The old couple just in front of her looked to be retired and had only two things that needed to be purchased. There were a few baskets ahead of the old couple, and the checker working the line was good and fast.

In no time at all, the old couple had laid their items on the counter, and were about to pay, when the old man said, "The newspaper says you have lettuce for sixty-nine cents. We couldn't find any there in the produce section. We want a rain check."

Dr. Michelle was in a hurry to get back to a sick horse. The last thing she needed was to wait for a rain check that would save someone twelve cents on lettuce. To make matters worse, the checker was out of rain checks at her cash register. She started walking from checker to checker, trying to find a rain check form to give to these people for sixty-nine-cent lettuce.

No one else had a rain check, so the checker had to go to the front office. Dr. Michelle looked around and discovered that she had actually chosen the slowest of all lines and that every customer who would have been behind her in line was already checked out and gone.

Just as she was about to offer the people a dollar if they'd just move on and let her check out, the much-anticipated rain check arrived. But instead of handing the rain check to the elderly couple, the checker started writing on it. It was a generic rain check, and the details about a product had to be filled in and signed by a manager. Of course, there was no manager around, so the checker had to get on the overhead loudspeaker and summon one to her register. Makes you want to pull your hair out just reading about it, doesn't it?

That feeling you're having is a lot like what a dog experiences when it chews its stitches out five minutes after it wakes up from surgery. Or a horse that kicks the stall wall over and over with the leg you spent all day putting a cast on. Maybe a cat that bites and scratches you every time you try to treat it for a disease that will be fatal if it doesn't take the medicine. Or a cow that runs you over and stomps on you while you're trying to deliver the calf that's stuck halfway in and halfway out. With veterinary patients, well, we kindly ask that you have just a little more patience.

Four

Veterinary (mis)Adventures

You can always tell a pioneer by the arrows in his ass.
—Dr. Chuck Deyhle, 1990

Brandon and the Fly

My brother is ten years younger than me, and his brain could eat my brain and not be full. He has more letters after his name than anyone I know. He is a professor at some institute of neurology and can say more big words in one sentence than anyone I have ever met. I was watching him in an interview on a *Good Morning America*–type show about the death of a celebrity and was amazed at how many adjectives came out of his mouth before he finally got to the noun they described.

As I watched the interview, my mind drifted back to watching him grow up and become a famous doctor who fixes people with broken brains. I thought, *We are very different.* I live in a tiny town in West Texas and try to avoid crowds of people at all costs; he lives in Dallas, Texas, and flies all over the world giving lectures on neurology.

As I watched him sittin' there all dressed up on TV, I remembered the times he would hang out with me at the vet clinic when he was a kid. He was still in high school when I moved to Lamesa, and he would spend days or weeks at a time working with me and getting a taste of rural America.

During one visit, when we made a call to an ostrich farm of all places, I would have sworn Brandon wasn't all that bright. The ostrich farmers were having some trouble with their chicks becoming crippled and called me out to have a look. I took Brandon with me because I knew we were gonna have to do some running to catch these birds, and he was a fast rascal.

The baby ostriches lived in pens about thirty feet long and maybe fifteen feet wide. There were little fences about three feet high between the pens, and each pen held ten ostriches. The owner of these ostriches was a detail man. He wanted everything just right and kept things so neat and clean that you could eat off the floor. They had giant incubators and barns built with heated floors and central air.

After the owner gave us an extensive history of the problem, I sent Brandon into the pen and told him to catch one of the crippled birds and bring it over to us so we could have a look.

Well, Brandon immediately went into overdrive. He hopped over the short fence with nothing on his mind but catching the ostrich we had identified. He was so focused that he didn't see the super-sticky fly tape thingy that was hanging down into the pen. In fact, he didn't see any of the numerous super-sticky fly tape thingies hanging into the pen.

Brandon hit the first one with the top of his head. The next one caught him on the front of his shirt, and the third one across his forehead. Those things are so darn sticky that, once they make contact, they will stay with you no matter what.

It was the impact and adherence of that third one to his forehead that brought him to a standstill. He reached up to attempt to pull it off, never considering that it would also stick to his hand when he touched it. As he tried and tried to pull it off, it just moved a bit until it was over his eyes and sticking to his eyebrows and eyelashes. Still not processing the degree of stick, he reached his other hand to release the one stuck to the top of his head.

Imagine the scene: Brandon's right hand was stuck to the fly tape that was also stuck to his eyes. His left hand was stuck to the fly tape that was also stuck in his hair. Attempts to pull on either one resulted in hair-pulling pain and no apparent way to escape. Not only that, but he could no longer see, so he ran into the wall and stuck to it by the tape that was bound to his shirt and neck.

He hollered for help, but he wasn't gonna get it from me. I wasn't going to touch him because sticky stuff like that grosses me out. The owner dude must have felt the same because he just stood there, too. Brandon was pleading with us to get the fly tape off him gently, but neither of us was able to do anything but laugh.

Finally, we got some rags and managed to pull all the tape off his body. He hollered for us to slow down while we pulled off the strips attached to his hair and eyebrows, but we assured him that ripping it off in one fast motion would be less painful.

Brandon could barely open his eyes on the way home because the residual sticky stuff had matted his eyelashes together.

And look at him now, I thought. He was on TV, saying more big words than anyone I have ever known.

Big White Bull

I was running as fast as I could when the big white bull's head made contact with my right butt cheek. I remember being surprised by its gentleness as it moved up the back of my thigh. But that didn't last long. It was quickly replaced with incredible force—the kind that makes you suddenly feel small—like a little kid playing with Dad, or a skier being pulled out of the water by a motorboat.

A false sense of security had lured me into the predicament at hand. Most bulls will either run you out of the pen to begin with or put up with you to the end. Not this one! He started off just fine and then turned into the devil. He had decided it was time to rid the pen of the scoundrel veterinarian who kept touching his recently acquired boo-boo. He had put up with me for three or four minutes, but now I had to go.

The bull's connection with the wallet in my left back pocket must have caused his adrenal glands to contract, fueling him with a burst of energy that sent me flying. The weight ratio of bull to man is about ten to one—his two thousand pounds to my two hundred launched me into the air.

My next sensation was *almost* pleasant. Weightlessness is surely more enjoyable when it is not interrupted by thoughts of "How high am I going to go?" and "Where am I going to land?" My legs and arms flailed, fruitlessly grabbing at air as I tried to position myself to absorb the impact of landing in the least painful manner. Midair calculations told me that if the fence was five feet tall, I must have been ten or twelve feet in the air as I sailed over it. I was much higher than the cab of my pickup—in fact, I was easily clearing the cab of my pickup.

What was in the back of my pickup? I wondered, as my calculations had me traveling right into the bed.

Then I remembered: pig feed! I had just loaded eight fifty-pound bags of pig feed into the bed of the truck and they were, for once, actually lying perfectly flat. I was thanking myself for taking a little extra time to load them in an organized manner as the bed came into view.

Oh my! I had forgotten about the shovel! There it was, sharp side up and poised to strike like a hissing snake. It was the last thing I had put in and was, of course, on top of the soft sacks of pig feed. My hands and head were coming in first. All I would have to do was give the shovel a quick shove and then roll over on my shoulder, and all would be well.

I could hear the spectators making that sound—a gasp coupled with a sudden inhale—that people make when they just know something awful is about to happen.

Thank goodness, the shovel had slid forward a bit when I stopped the truck. This left me about two feet of space to reach my hands out and push the shovel out of the way. Or so I thought. Of course, I missed, but the motion to push the shovel caused me to roll up into a neat ball, which was the form I took as I landed, wedged between the tailgate and the last feed sack.

The crowd moved in to see if I was alive. I let out a few moans as I began to uncoil, assessing my body for damage. My head had narrowly missed the shovel and, as far as I could tell, everything still moved and was still attached. I lay there for a minute, listening as the group reenacted the event and marveled at the luck of landing on that pig feed and pondering why anyone would go to school for eight years to spend their days in a bull pen.

When I was back on my feet, we took the bull to the clinic. My time in the pen was over.

Mystery

The directions I held in my hand were leading me into a residential area in Lubbock, Texas. That would not have been a big deal were it not for the fact that I was on my way to see to a new client—a horse. I figured people in an urban neighborhood were as likely to know as much about horses as I knew about submarines.

The plan was to call the client and tell him when I would arrive so he could meet me. I would palpate his horse to see if she was pregnant. It turned out that he had an appointment and could not be there, which left me alone to catch and palpate a perfect stranger's horse. I did not like how this was going.

I arrived at a brick home with a large backyard. A row of eight-foot-tall sheds separated the yard from the horses in the lot next door. I had been instructed to pull into the alley and enter through the back gate. I was also told that a halter would be tied to the fence and there were stocks where I could restrain the mare to palpate her.

Of course, I could not locate the stocks, and the only thing tied to the fence was a lead rope. To make matters worse, there were four horses in the round pen. Have you ever tried to catch one of four horses that are running around a circular track? It's pretty much impossible; they stayed on the opposite side of that round pen no matter what I did.

So, I did what any industrious vet would do: I set about building a barrier that would stop them. It took about fifteen minutes of Aggie ingenuity, but I managed it. I finally got them cornered and picked out the only mare in the bunch. She was a wild thing! I got the lead rope around her neck, only to find that she didn't like that at all! She reared and pitched a fit.

As I tried to calm her, I heard a voice from the adjoining backyard: "Hello?"

The voice was a welcome melody at a trying moment. I began to reply in a fervent tone.

"Yes, I'm Dr. Brock, and I'm here to palpate this mare. Could you please tell me where a halter might be?"

I was speaking in a tone somewhere between yelling and civil conversation. I meant to be polite yet convey a sense of aggravation over the unorganized state in which I found myself.

"Hello?" was all I got in response.

I started analyzing the voice to see if I could get an idea of who might be beckoning me. The tone sounded a bit like an older woman wondering who was in the yard chasing the horses.

I changed my tone a bit, adding a little more volume and a little more respect.

"Yes, I'm Dr. Brock, and I have come to see if this mare is pregnant. I was told there were stocks around here that I could use to restrain her. Do you know where the rest of this halter is?"

Several minutes of silence passed, making me wonder just how old this woman might be. In my mind I pictured a gray-haired woman inching across the yard with her walker, trying to adjust her hearing aid, wondering who was kicking up all the dust. I decided to raise my volume a little more and add more respect.

"Yes, I'm Dr. Brock, and I was needing—"

Before I could get any more words out, I heard a remark that made me wonder if the old lady might be getting a bit senile.

"Well, my stars!"

What on earth does that mean? It seemed like a poor conversational placement for those words.

My grandmothers always used nonsensical expressions like that— things like "land o' Goshen" and "well, forevermore." They said phrases such as, "well, for Pete's sake" and "for the love of Pete." (Who the heck is Pete, anyway?) This further raised my suspicion that the speaker must be an old woman.

I decided to tie the horse to the fence and speak to this woman face-to-face. But there was no one in the yard. No one! There were no footprints in the dirt, no evidence of anyone with a walker. The back door was locked tight, and no one was visible through the back windows. Was I was dreaming? Losing my mind? Hearing things? Was someone deliberately messing with me? That'd be a pretty mean joke to play on a vet you've never met before.

Just as I was about to reach the end of the row of sheds and return to the lot full of horses, I heard the voice again: "Hello?"

It was that moment that I realized it was originating in a thicket of trees in the opposite corner of the lot. I made my way over and parted the vegetation.

And, there she was. Not the little old lady I expected, but a large blue macaw parrot.

I had just carried on a twenty-minute conversation with a bird. I quickly scanned the area to make sure no one had just seen or heard me make an idiot of myself.

After I recovered from my humiliation, I found the stocks and managed to get the mare into them. She was in foal.

Having done my job, I promptly got out of there before someone showed up and that bird told him how dumb the new veterinarian was.

———

I have never been able to do this story justice in retelling it. When I figured out what had just happened, I laughed hysterically as I gawked at that dang bird.

I have rewritten this story four times trying to convey the emotion I went through to anyone who might read it. I don't think I'll ever get it right. When you spend twenty minutes believing that you are conversing with a human only to find out that you have been talking to a bird, it's kinda like stepping off a curb, stumbling, then recovering, only to play it off as you scan around to make sure no one witnessed your blunder.

Goose

I often think *Crocodile Dundee* has nothing on veterinarians. We never know what the day holds, and sometimes it holds more than we expect.

I got a call about a down cow. She had gone down sometime in the night and couldn't get back up. It's a frequent issue with cows, and it's one of the most common reasons I make farm calls.

When I left the clinic, I figured this cow would be fixed up with no trouble and I'd be back in a short while. The owner informed me that he would not be there but described in detail where the cow was.

I arrived and found things just as the owner had described them. I went through a gate and approached a run-down barn with chicken-wire pens all around it. It was obvious that the place had not been well cared for over the years.

There were animals of all kinds. I saw goats, peacocks, and pigs just running around loose, horses, barking dogs, rabbits in cages, chickens of all sizes and breeds, sheep, a llama, and a few dairy cows.

I had been informed that the cow would be just past the gate, beyond the water trough, after I walked through the barn.

I made my way to the barn and came to an incredible realization. The manure in the barn had piled up so much over the years that I had to stoop over to walk through. There must have been manure ten feet deep covering the floor. I squatted down and began the trek, carrying the few things that I thought I might need to work on the cow. The farther I went, the lower the clearance. By the time I reached the middle of the barn, I had to get on my hands and knees to clear the rafters!

By about halfway through, I heard a loud noise coming from my left side. It was a gurgled, hissing sound accompanied by the sound of flat feet slapping damp ground. It was very dark in that direction, so I could not make out what was responsible for the sound. My mind raced as I anticipated a strange creature emerging into the few columns of dim light that pierced the darkness of the barn.

Until you are wedged between a ten-foot manure pile and a barn roof, you never realize how menacingly large a male goose is. In fact, as this monster came into focus, he appeared to be five feet tall! This goose had teeth, and a massive horn in the middle of his head—or at least it appeared this way from my vantage point.

I found myself once again assessing my supplies to determine what I could best use as a weapon to defend myself. The goose was coming fast, and he meant business. He brought with him an angry entourage of six female geese defending his flanks.

I reached into my bag and retrieved a plastic bottle of glucose. I gripped it tightly in my right hand and prepared for the worst. I was wondering how much of this goose was bluff and how much was really fight. He answered my question a second later, spreading his wings just before he gave me a mighty peck on the side of my head and the brim of my cap. The entire time, he made a wicked hissing sound, as the female chorus spread out and honked endlessly from all directions.

The repeated pecks to my head only served to change my initial fear to anger. It hurt just enough to make me mad. But I didn't know what to do. I didn't want to hurt him, but I didn't want to keep taking a head peckin', either!

By now, the goose army had backed me into a corner. The noise level was remarkable as they honked and hissed at the intruder. Here I was, in a barn full of dookie being attacked by a gaggle of geese. I was unable to stand, had nothing to defend myself with but a bottle of glucose, and was afraid of hurting them if I retaliated too harshly.

I decided to try the "get big and get loud" approach, hoping this would scare them off. I got as tall as the area allowed and screamed, "Get outta here, goose!" at the top of my lungs. It worked! The geese took off toward the door, flapping and honking as they went.

They paused just beyond the shadow of the door and looked at me. As long as I was still, they were quiet and stayed away. If I made a movement to gather my things or head toward the door, they would honk and charge me. This went on for a few minutes while I hatched a plan. Finally, I decided simply to get up and go to the cow. If they got in my way, I would just run over them.

I began to make my way in the direction of the cow. This infuriated them, of course, and they ran and hissed at me with all they had. I plowed through them like a fullback and made it out of the barn and to the side of the cow.

I began my usual down-cow procedure. A curious dog ambled over to investigate the situation, only to be chased off by the giant, horned goose. It was very apparent that this goose ruled the farm. The treatment included a bottle of fluid to be given intravenously at a slow rate. I sat by that cow's side for thirty minutes and defended myself from an attack army of geese. They never left, and I never gave up.

By the time I returned to the clinic, I felt like I had boxed twelve rounds. I decided I would rather combat a mad dog than face a herd of angry geese in a manure-filled barn.

Skunked

"I told Papa not to throw them scraps off the back porch," a voice whined on the other end of the phone.

It was Mrs. Olgien, and her tone conveyed her remorse for calling me on Christmas Eve tinged with her anger at Papa for being too lazy to walk out to the chicken yard. I had never met them or been to their house. It was my first Christmas as a veterinarian—I might as well embark on another adventure.

Cold doesn't even begin to describe the effects that a twenty-five-mile-per-hour north wind had on the rolling canyons of Clarendon, Texas. I was dreading leaving the warmth of the house for what seemed like such a petty call.

The combination of scraps and warmth under the Olgiens' house had lured a skunk. Somehow this critter had wedged himself between two footers under the house and become very stuck. The family, fortunately, had discovered the culprit without causing him to deploy his stink bomb. I had been brought in to sedate the skunk and carefully remove him from his predicament.

I was still new in the community and very much wanted to please these people and perhaps make some new friends and clients.

The Olgiens lived twenty miles from the closest anywhere, and there must have been ten cars parked around this house. A combination of family in for Christmas and neighbors had made this home the hot ticket for Christmas Eve. One of the cars in the yard had the insignia of the Donley County Sheriff's Department, indicating that even the law had come to visit.

I parked about a hundred yards from the house and the walk allowed me to focus on my mission and be thankful that the house faced north and the skunk was under the back porch.

As I the festively illuminated front door came into view, I noticed the womenfolk were gathered in the front room. None of the men were in sight.

"You better get in here, Dr. Bo," Mamma Olgien greeted me at the door, her voice more toned down than when she called. "The men are in the backyard trying to figure out how to get the varmint."

I was quickly introduced to everyone in the room and then escorted out back.

Fifteen men stood in the backyard, sizing me up as I exited the house with Mamma. After a thorough briefing, I scooted under the porch toward a two-foot-square opening that led into the crawl space under the house. Upon peering into the darkness, I caught my first glimpse of the skunk's fanny. It was not at all how I had pictured the situation. The skunk was about seven feet away, really wedged between two footers. There was no way I could get a shot of sedative into one of those buns and then get away before the stink bomb exploded.

I backed out, and conferred with the men. We decided to reach in with a syringe taped to the end of a broom. The small needle might just be gentle enough to keep the skunk from spraying, but just in case, I would be a long way off.

I filled the syringe with about twice the dose of sedative that I would have given a cat. I felt like G. I. Joe as I belly crawled, inch by inch, toward the trespasser. Carefully glancing around the protection of the footer, I gently inserted the tiny needle into the left bun of the skunk and slipped him a Mickey. Not a whiff of odor entered the air. What an accomplishment! I scurried out to a hero's welcome. I felt sure I would be profiled on *Wild Kingdom* after such a successful mission.

The whole crowd of us went back into the house to enjoy a cup of Mamma's hot chocolate as we waited for the sedative to take effect. We visited and laughed for a few minutes, and then I began to make my hero's departure.

I was about to leave when Mamma asked if we had actually removed the now-snoring skunk.

"No," I answered, but I assured her that it would just take a second, and I would do it before I left.

A few of the men went out with me as I crawled back under the house to dislodge the sleeping skunk.

I peered in at the now-limp tail of the skunk and quickly closed the seven-foot gap that separated us. I pulled and tugged with little success. The thing was wedged much harder than I had figured. By now, about thirty minutes had passed since the shot.

When the skunk finally came free, our eyes met. It was at this moment that I realized that the drug had worn off.

This critter had been wedged between boards, injected with a needle, and had never released a drop of liquid stink. But the minute our eyes met, he let loose. He got me right on the side of the head. Forgetting my confines of my space and reacting on pure instinct, I jumped back, banging my head on the floor above me.

By this time, only the toughest of the bunch remained in the yard. They knew before I backed out that the mission had taken a serious turn for the worse. I could hear the sheriff saying something about clearing the area and forming a perimeter.

My eyes were watering so badly, I was blinded. The smell of roadkill skunk is bad, but the smell of freshly deployed skunk bomb actually hurts, especially when it's up close and personal.

It was then that I felt something warm and liquid running down my neck. Have I mentioned that I can't stand to see my own blood? That's right. I can do a C-section on a cow and then have a hamburger for dinner, but the steady flow of my own blood is sure to make me pass out.

Maybe I'm a sissy, but I have no control over it. I can take kicks, cuts, and contusions just fine, but bleeding takes me down.

My knuckles were white as I held tight to Mr. Skunk. I never let go as I backed out from under the porch. I emerged into a ring of people I had never met, holding a skunk by its tail on Christmas Eve, on the verge of passing out cold.

The next few scenes happened in slow motion. Everyone backed away as the smell engulfed the area. I heard someone say, "He's bleeding all over the place," and I dropped to my knees and then face-planted, as if on cue.

I came to in the garage with Mamma rubbing my head with a cold rag.

I stank. The four men who had carried me to the garage stank, the women who had taken off my coat and boots stank, and my pickup stank for two months just from the drive home.

I took two baths in tomato juice but still had to sleep on a towel-covered couch for three days.

I talked to Mrs. Olgien a week or so later, and she told me that it still smelled in the house but that they had gotten used to it. They surely would have been better off had they never called me.

The moral of the story: don't visit too long on Christmas Eve after shooting a skunk with twice the cat dose of sedative. Merry Christmas, everyone.

The Old Man and the Tree

It was about closing time, and I was thinking how nice it would be to leave on time for a change. Then the phone rang.

The man on the other end of the line sounded like the oldest living man on earth.

He was trying to explain how his prize heifer was down having her calf, but he could barely complete a sentence before starting a different subject.

It was apparent that there was no way he could bring the cow in because she couldn't stand up, so I packed all the stuff I thought I might need and headed off with the worst set of directions imaginable.

By the time I arrived at the "ranch," it was pitch-dark and colder than a freezer.

I saw the old man standing next to a sky-blue 1977 pickup truck with a scrap-iron headache rack and one of those old, coiled CB antennas attached to the rack. He didn't even move when I left my vehicle and walked over to him. He was leaning against the pickup, his eyes closed. I stood right in front of him and finally came to the conclusion that he was asleep. Yep, that's right; he had dozed off while standing.

I spoke a few words at a moderate volume. Nothing. I raised my voice a bit, and this roused him.

"I'm Dr. Brock, and I have come to deliver your calf," poured from my mouth in that I-am-talking-to-an-old-man volume and tone.

This only made him bring a cupped hand to his ear and utter a hearty, "Huh?"

I repeated myself at near-screaming level.

"Oh, it's not my heifer; it's Daddy's," he said.

Did I hear correctly? This guy still has a living father and he owns the cattle?

As if on cue, the passenger door of the pickup opened, and "Daddy" slid out. He was bent into a permanent comma, with about fifty gray hairs growing from a single spot in the middle of his head, and he had no teeth. He wore overalls and no coat.

Then the driver's door opened, and Ol' Sleepy's brother climbed out.

Not a one of them could hear and they all talked at the same time. I gathered from the chatter that the cow was out in the pasture and that they wanted me to get my stuff and ride in the back of their truck. Off we went.

My technician, Manda, had come along, so I asked her to follow us in my truck outside the fence. I would call her on the cell phone if we needed anything.

We drove into the darkness for what seemed like an hour and

finally found the heifer. She was on her side with just the head of the calf sticking out. I jumped out with a rope to tie her so we could pull the calf, but the second she saw me, she jumped up and ran off.

Now imagine the scene: I'm in the middle of a five-square-mile pasture with three guys who are clinically deaf, trying to catch a crazed heifer and deliver a calf. Furthermore, it seems I am going to have to rope the critter from the back of a '77 pickup with Daddy at the wheel.

The heifer headed for a draw with a thick stand of salt cedars in it, so I really needed to get that rope on her fast. Daddy must have noticed this too, because he gunned the truck and brought me in perfect position to toss my loop. Surprisingly, I caught her on the first throw.

Now what? There was nothing to attach the rope to except that wire-loop CB antenna. It was well anchored to the headache rack—so much so that when the cow hit the end of the rope—the antenna held firm. Unfortunately, the headache rack didn't. It flew out of the truck bed as the heifer kept running, dragging my rope, the CB antenna, and the headache rack, with the old man hot on her trail.

As luck would have it, she got the entire contraption lodged in the first tree she passed. This stopped her and gave me time to jump out. I'm not sure what I thought I was going to do with a thousand-pound cow on the end of a rope hung up in a four-foot cedar sapling, but jumping out of the truck bed seemed like the thing to do.

When she saw me, she started circling the tree. This prompted Daddy, for some reason, to start chasing her around the tree in the truck.

"Stop chasing her," I yelled, waving my arms.

He heard nothing, and just kept driving around the sapling in smaller and smaller circles until he finally went right over the top of it. The front of the truck made it over the tree, but when the back end was directly on top of it, it lifted the rear of the truck right off the ground.

The fact that he'd stopped moving made the old man press harder on the gas pedal, spinning the tires a million miles an hour. The engine screamed like a jet, but he had no idea what was going on.

I was standing in front of the truck thinking that, if that little tree broke, I would surely die. I jumped out of the way just in time to hear it snap and see that sky-blue pickup take off like a jet from an aircraft carrier.

In less than a second, the truck disappeared into the cedar thicket, but then the motor died, and things got very quiet. I heard the doors open, and in a few minutes, they all meandered out.

The cow was gone.

I called Manda to come and get us. We drove back to their house listening to them all talk at once about the adventure. I called them several times the next day but never got an answer.

As far as I know, that truck is still in the cedars, and my rope is still attached to the cow.

The Old Man and the Open Cows

I can remember looking down and seeing 8:02 on the digital clock in the pickup as I pulled up to the ranch.

I use the term "ranch" loosely because this gentleman had only seventeen cows. That doesn't really mean ranch in West Texas.

It was going to be a busy morning at the clinic, so with any luck, I would be back by nine o'clock and could start getting caught up. After all, how long could it take to palpate seventeen cows for pregnancy? At some of the ranches we go to, we palpate 750 to 800 head in a day.

I had never met this fellow but I wasn't surprised to see that he was old. His voice on the phone sounded like each breath might be his last. I watched him mosey out of a stucco house that hadn't been painted or repaired in any way for at least fifty years. He was about six foot five and weighed about 125 pounds. He was so thin and wore such tight jeans that it looked as if his legs bent four or five times before they connected with his feet. He was wearing one of those Western shirts with snaps for buttons and had a giant bandana tied around his neck. His boots were straight out of a grade-B Western movie. They were so pointy that his toes just had to be sitting one atop the other in order to conform to the angle.

The only piece of attire that did not fit the Western motif was his hat—it looked like the one that the engineer on *Petticoat Junction* wore. It was made out of striped mattress ticking and was so worn that it had taken on a lean to the left side of his head.

He didn't speak a word as he approached. He just pointed over to a set of run-down sheds and a working pen about the size of a football field.

I put the pickup in drive and headed over as he ambled across the yard at a snail's pace and began to talk long before I could hear what he was saying.

I began to size up the situation. Seventeen cows of various sizes and shapes stood in the middle of a one-acre trap. In the center of the trap was the oldest squeeze chute I had ever seen. There were no alleys leading to the chute at all. It just sat like a centerpiece on a Thanksgiving table. In fact, there was no fence in the entire trap, except the one that made up the perimeter.

It was obvious that he had coaxed the cattle in from a large pasture that was beyond the south end of the trap. These cows did not look like they had been handled much. They were looking at me with wide nostrils and high heads.

He was still mumbling as he approached, but I was not concerned with what he was saying. I was concentrating on the logistics of an eighty-year-old man and a thirty-five-year-old veterinarian getting seventeen snorting cows through a squeeze chute with no alleys leading to it. I was beginning to think that this was going to put me a little behind on the tidy schedule the secretary had booked for the day.

When his ramblings finally penetrated the wall of my thoughts, it became apparent that one of the cows might be a little dangerous. He called the red one "a bit snakey." Having been around old cowboy dudes all my life, I know what "snakey" means: it means look out! He was not kidding, either. That damn cow would leave the herd and charge anything that came into the pen.

So we came up with a plan: Grandpa and I were going to carry twenty pipe panels (each weighing about three hundred pounds each) from the barn (a hundred yards away) to construct an alley into the antique chute, all while dodging the "snakey" red cow.

Well, it took this old coot a full five minutes to walk across the yard. It was becoming clear that I would be more than a little behind when I got back to the clinic.

The red, glowing letters on the dash of the pickup said 10:29 as I plopped into the seat for a drink of water. It had only taken two and a half hours to "throw up a few panels." My back was aching and my patience was shot.

To make matters worse, the red cow liked the old man. It was me she wanted to charge. She would run back and forth around him, and he would never even change expressions. But she must have blown two gallons of snot on me; I must have kicked two tons of dirt on her.

If those panels weighed 300 pounds apiece, I carried 285 pounds, and he carried fifteen. But that was not the bad part. Because he walked so slowly, I had to bear 285 pounds for about five times longer than I would have if I had pulled each one of them over by myself. Oh, but he insisted on helping.

The clock in the pickup read 12:02 as I sat in the front seat wondering why not one cow was pregnant. He had "run" up to the house to get some paperwork, while I wondered how I was going to salvage the rest of the day. By now, most of the early appointments had probably left, and the later ones were pacing the floor and calling me names.

To make matters worse, I had mashed my right index finger in the mechanical squeeze chute while maneuvering the cows into the chute. The process was repetitive, but not without its dangers. I would push the cattle up, catch the head, squeeze the chute, open the tailgate, put a pipe behind each one, palpate her, mark her with a paint stick, and finally let her go. The rancher's contribution to the entire process was to give me a verbal history of every cow.

When he finally returned, I told him that since every cow was open, we should really test his bull.

To this he replied, "What bull? I ain't got no bull. Haven't had one in over a year!"

I could feel my blood pressure rising. What in the world was this guy thinking? I spent all morning palpating cows that he said should have been calving three months ago, only to find out that he doesn't even have a bull. I was about to explode with some "anger-inspired" statements, when he interrupted me with a quote that I will never forget: "I don't need no bull. Been feedin' 'em them there breeder's cubes for about a year now."

Oh my, I thought over and over as I drove back to the clinic. *Three dollars a head*, crossed my mind a few times as I cruised along. That's right. All I would have to show for that morning's effort was fifty-one bucks plus a small call fee.

It had crossed my mind as we constructed the working pens that none of those cows looked pregnant. It had crossed my mind a few times that there was no bull around. It had crossed my mind a few times that I should have been getting a history while we worked. But it never crossed my mind that anyone would ever think that "breeder's cubes" would impregnate a cow!

HIpple

The foal was in bad shape when it arrived from three hours away. It had colicked, and all the tests looked bad. As if that wasn't enough reason to be bummed out, the owners were oddballs. The woman was a card-carrying hippie, and her boyfriend was wearing a do-rag with a sports coat and cutoff jeans. And to top that off, they were obsessive-compulsive about the foal, asking questions so fast I didn't have time to answer the first before they started in on the second.

I can deal with badly colicked foals, but crazy owners who won't quit asking questions and worry about tiny details drive me nuts. After dealing with them for twenty-two years, I have lost all patience. These people may have been the worst I have ever seen. They wanted to stand in the surgery room while the surgery was going on. I politely told them that there was a big window that looked into the horse surgery room, and they could watch through that.

I informed the veterinarian running anesthesia that I did not want this foal getting too deep. There are many valid scientific reasons to keep foals in this condition from getting overanesthetized, and I had a serious look on my face as we entered surgery and I told her this. She followed my instructions to a T. There were several times during the surgery that the foal became a little light, but I didn't complain. I didn't want its blood pressure or cardiac output compromised.

The surgery went well. We found the problem and corrected it in short order. I told the crew, as I left it with them to close the incision, that I did not want this critter dying from anesthesia.

The foal's owners greeted me outside the surgery room in front of the window with a thousand more questions, just as I expected. The hippie woman was now mad at the do-rag-wearing boyfriend because he was asking questions faster than she was, and I just stood there watching them argue over whose turn it was to ramble meaningless questions that had no answer.

As luck would have it, they were standing with their backs to the window, and I was facing them. I noticed all the people in the surgery room suddenly begin moving quickly with deliberate intent. I noticed that the foal was moving on the table. It was waking up before they had time to get it off the table, which was both good and bad. Good because it was not going to die from the effects of the anesthesia; bad because if these people turned around and saw that baby moving on the table, *they* were gonna prolapse.

All of the people in the surgery room were looking at me with huge eyes. I could tell they all realized the magnitude of the situation. Somehow, I never changed expressions. Don't ask me how; I don't usually have a poker face at all. I even managed to use only my peripheral vision to assess the situation. I never lost eye contact with the bickering duo.

When they began to turn their bodies to a position that might allow the motion in the surgery room to grab their attention, I leapt into action.

Instead of listening to their questions, I began to volley a continuous stream of meaningless questions at them. While rattling off these questions, I got louder, more serious, and gradually moved to my right, which made them turn their backs to the window once again. I wouldn't even let them finish answering a question before I bellowed out the next one with even more conviction in my voice and my eyebrows higher on my forehead. This seemed to be just what they longed for. They were hypnotized by my tone and facial expressions. They were digging deep into their gray matter for equally explosive answers.

This went on for a good five minutes, until the surgery crew could get the foal into the recovery room. When the door shut behind them, my face immediately returned to its typical expressionless skin bag with many eye wrinkles. They seemed to be disappointed—in fact, they both paused for a moment and looked into the now-empty surgery room, as if for more drama.

"Wow, we were so involved in the conversation, I didn't even see them take our foal out of the room. I sure hope she wakes up soon. Anesthesia is the scariest part of surgery, you know."

I could hear laughter coming from the lab that adjoins the exam room in which I was talking to these people. I knew what they were laughing about, even though I couldn't make out a word they were saying. I eventually sent the couple on their way and got to rehash the entire event from the other side of the window. The crew was more proud of me for managing to keep those people from seeing the pandemonium than for anything I have done before or since.

I love my job.

—— *Five* ——

Adventures in the Field

*Always look for the obvious, Big Doctor. If you find
something else, they will name it after you.*
—Dr. Chuck Deyhle, 1990

The minute you leave the clinic you're like a sailor overboard. At least, that's how I feel.

Some veterinarians don't even have a clinic, they just drive from place to place working on animals and doing their thing. I have never been that way; I like to have everything in one place and to manage several patients at the same time. You can't do that when you're out on a call. But unfortunately, sometimes you just have to go and you just never know what's going to happen or how you'll adapt to it.

Hopefully stories of my veterinary (mis)adventures will give you the feel of what it is like leaving the comfort of the clinic and entering the unpredictable world of the farm call.

Boxer Shorts

I have always heard about hog operations in the Upper Midwest but hadn't been to one until recently. These places are the pinnacle of science and agriculture. The pigs are genetically programmed to grow fast and efficiently while resisting many diseases. Disease resistance doesn't keep these hog farmers from being sticklers for cleanliness, though; oh no, they are germ nuts. That's right, they don't want even one germ to enter their pig facilities. This is where the story starts.

One of my hosts at this vet clinic in the Upper Midwest had been so kind as to arrange a tour of one of the farrowing facilities in his practice. I was looking forward to experiencing high-tech pig production at its finest. On the trip over, he explained the production expectations of such an operation: fifteen hundred sows in one building having litters 2.5 times per year, weaning about twenty-six pigs per sow per year. Wow, that is making some pork. I was anxious to see how all this worked as we pulled into the farm.

As we entered the front door of the farrowing facility, I estimated the building to be about the size of a football field. It was quite, clean, odorless, and well kept. The first person we encountered as we entered the reception area was the owner of the facility. She was a kind-looking woman with a wonderful smile and an extremely Midwestern accent.

"Glad to see ya. You guys grab a shower and come on in," were her opening words from the "germ-free" area.

I had heard about this shower thing but had never actually done it. This is a requirement for anyone who enters one of these high-tech facilities. You have to take off all of your clothes, take a shower (including washing your hair), and change into germ-free clothes provided for you on the other side of the shower.

After the other vet went through, a red light came on indicating that it was my turn. The first little room was separated from the second little room by a shower. I was to take off all of my clothes and take a shower. *No big deal,* I thought, *I'll just hang my clothes here and hop into this shower.* So I did.

The problem came when I entered the next little room on the other side of the shower. Here I was, totally naked, and there it was, a pile of underwear. Now, I feel strongly that underwear is just not one of those things that people share. What should I do? It kinda gave me the willies. Where exactly did these underwear come from? Had they been worn by others? Did they go to Walmart and buy a variety pack? Sheesh.

I started considering what qualities I would like in a pair of underwear that had recently covered the fanny of a total stranger. After a moment of sorting, it became apparent that size was the major issue. Big, that's right, the bigger the better. In fact, so big that they actually touch nothing except the waist. And there they were, a pair of argyle boxers big enough for an offensive lineman for the Minnesota Vikings. Inspection of the tag in the band revealed a waist size of fifty-two.

I slid into them and then put on a pair of coveralls. The rest of my trip through the hog facility was spent listening with one ear while trying to keep the size-fifty-two boxers from sliding off. I kept one hand in my pocket, clutching that waistband, for as long as possible.

Finally, a situation arrived that required both of my hands. The boxers immediately fell down to the inseam of the also-oversized coveralls. There is no way to pull up a pair of size-fifty-two boxers once they have fallen without taking off the coveralls, so I decided to just leave them alone and make the best of it.

As far as I know, no one could tell it happened. The only effect it had on me was a great reduction in my stride length. I had to take about two steps to their one for the rest of the tour.

The moral of the story is this: Always carry an extra pair of my own, autoclaved underwear.

"Ze Liver from ze Duck"

I drive nine miles to and from my office every day. It's nine miles of road so flat and treeless that, on a dark night, you can see the lights from towns fifteen or twenty miles away. The people around here drive pickups and talk about tractors and horses. A night on the town means making a sixty-mile trip to Lubbock to take in some barbecue and a movie. It's who we are and what we do in Lamesa, and I just figured the whole world was that way, too.

A few years back, I was asked to sit on an advisory board for a pharmaceutical company. This was, of course, quite an honor, and it meant spending some time in the Northeast to attend meetings.

I prepared to leave for my first meeting. The plane tickets had arrived, along with the hotel reservations and papers for car rental. The company was even footing the bill for Kerri (my wife) to come along.

We arrived at our destination and made it to the hotel. It was so big that it could sleep the entire town of Lamesa. The company spared no expense: the room had two bathrooms, unlimited room service, candy on the pillow, and very impressive dining options.

We were told that a car would pick us up and take us to our dinner spot to meet the rest of the board. I told Kerri that we might want to dress up a little. She put on a nice pantsuit, and I slipped into a pair of khakis and a pressed Wrangler 20X shirt. Our driver met us in the hotel lobby and drove us in a limousine about three blocks to a French restaurant.

We were seated with the others on the advisory board, all of whom were wearing suits and ties or evening dresses. "Uncomfortable" was the word that kept coming to mind as they brought us menus and filled our water glasses. The people seated around us were strangers, and not one of them looked as though he or she could discuss tractors or horses.

I unfolded my menu, but I couldn't read it. It was written in French. I sat there a minute and tried to think if I knew any French words. Hmmmm . . . nope . . . not one . . . not even a cuss word. Kerri made the discovery about the same time I did and started kicking me gently under the table.

Not wanting to appear any more ignorant than I already did in my khakis and white socks, I smiled at the waiter and pointed to two items on the menu. He graciously jotted something down for our orders.

"What did you get us?" Kerri asked out of the corner of her mouth as the tuxedo-clad waiter made his way around to the rest of our party.

"I have no idea," I muttered under my breath. "Just smile and eat it when it gets here."

About twenty minutes later, the food arrived. My plate had two brown piles of something surrounded by some green leaves. The food on Kerri's plate was red and the waiter struck a match to it. It burned brightly for about fifteen seconds before it went out.

As bad as the conversation was, it was pleasant compared to the food. I could barely choke down whatever was on my plate. When no one was looking, Kerri slipped her meal into her purse. I paid close attention to how much space she had left in her bag, but I was out of luck; it was full. I continued to eat and disguise my grimace.

When the evening finally ended, I asked the waiter on my way to the door what we had eaten. He smiled and said Kerri had some sort of raw fish. I had "ze liver from ze duck."

Wow, what are the odds of randomly pointing out the two things that we would never eat under normal circumstances? It made me wish for nine miles of flat road and a sixty-mile trip to Lubbock, where I can read the menu, wear white socks, and use my wife's purse for nonperishable items.

Buddy

A dog that lives at a veterinary clinic quite possibly enjoys the best of all canine lifestyles. Think about it: it has a built-in health-care policy; it meets every dog in town; it gets to bark at and chase cattle as they are loaded and unloaded; and it gets to eat the leftovers.

That's right: at the clinic, there are a ton of body parts at the end of the day. There are horns from dehorning, placentas from birthing, hooves from horseshoeing, and—perhaps best of all—oysters from castrations.

Buddy was our first clinic dog. He was an eighty-pound Airedale terrier that never knew anything other than the life of a vet-clinic dog.

I think he may still hold the world record for the number of oysters eaten in one day: fifty-four. Makes those guys who swallowed goldfish in their college days seem like amateurs.

I decided that Buddy needed a bit of culture outside of the clinic, so I began taking him to obedience school when he was about a year old. This, of course, was not his favorite thing to do. It involved discipline and dedication, two qualities that running free in the clinic had not instilled in him. At first, just the sight of that leash sent his tail between his legs and elicited a most pitiable facial expression.

The lessons were every Thursday night at the local fairgrounds. It was a group class, with about fifteen dogs at each meeting. Buddy learned to sit, stay, and come. He advanced to lying down and following at the perfect distance. Learning quickly and remembering well, Buddy was a star.

He exceeded my expectations until about the fifth lesson, when he seemed to have a lapse of reason. It was as though he suddenly forgot everything he had learned.

At the start of each class, we would all walk around in circles, teams of handlers and dogs marching one behind the other. It was sort of a warm-up to get the dogs tuned in and ready to have a lesson.

That fifth lesson found Buddy with no sense at all. He fought the leash, tried to sniff all the girl dogs, and growled at the boy dogs. He was driving me crazy, forcing me to pull on the choke chain with a bit more force than usual. That extra pressure made him cough and gag a bit, enough that he stopped and heaved up some of the day's prizes from the clinic.

Picture this: it was a cold winter night in a cavernous fair barn with fifteen dogs walking in a circle. There was not time for me to stop the parade to mop up a steaming pile of fresh mountain oysters, and the next dog in line is a two-pound Yorkie.

Suddenly I hear the woman behind me scream, "Oh my!" when she realized her Yorkie had something in his mouth. The oyster was nearly as big as he was and it was hanging out both sides of his mouth. He was as proud as a peacock.

We stopped the entire procession and went about trying to remove the Yorkie from the mountain oyster. Our valiant attempts were met with serious growls and a display of tiny teeth. The owner was beside herself. She had no idea where it had come from, and I was not about to claim responsibility.

It took quite a bit of work, but we finally got it away from him and resumed the lesson. As we marched back around toward the steaming pile, I was able to cover it with dirt to prevent another episode on the following lap.

I bet that to this day that woman has no idea what her little lapdog was gnawing on or where it came from. And, unless she reads this, she'll never learn it from me.

Buddy, A Eulogy

It is true that a veterinarian has to see the world through the eyes of an animal. For the past eight years, I have seen the world through the eyes of a big ol' Airedale named Buddy. He came to the clinic as a four-pound puppy and grew into an eighty-five-pound teddy bear that greeted every dog that came into the clinic with a friendly fanny sniff.

Buddy gave more than his weight in blood for transfusions and was a critical part of saving countless lives. He could pick out a lesion on an animal before I could even start the exam. If it was to be surgery on the back end, he would stand there and watch until he was pitched the results. Buddy has made friends with three dogcatchers and knew most everyone in Dawson and the surrounding counties.

But what I thank Buddy for is revealing to me the bond that makes people care so deeply for a critter. Because of him, I can cry when an elderly woman loses her best friend, a poodle she has had for fourteen years. Because of him, I go to extremes to make those last few months or years comfortable when a person has no one else to talk to all day long but an overweight Schnauzer. Because I saw the world through Buddy's eyes, I can see how people need pets to give them sunshine.

When the world has collapsed, and there's no love at all, there will still be the love of a dog. They just don't know otherwise. I've seen stoic old cowboys sob over the loss of dogs that helped them work and gave them smiles, stories, and a sympathetic ear. I've seen children's faces light up over a puppy that would love them without conditions.

Buddy died at five o'clock on Father's Day. I feel lost every time I castrate a horse and there is no Buddy to enjoy the rewards. I miss his powerful head nudging against my hand for a scratch. I've told stories of Buddy's adventures to six classes of vet students at Texas A&M and in several states. He had a wonderful personality and the patience of Job with small children and other animals. He loved people, and I know he loved me.

We will miss you, Buddy. Thanks for the sunshine.

One-Eyed Cow

Consider for a moment: How big is a fifteen-hundred-pound cow? Well, let me tell ya, it's about as large as the entire offensive line for the Dallas Cowboys. It weighs as much as half a car or about five refrigerators. That's a lot of body mass to be governed by such a small brain.

Discovering the force of such an animal is almost a rite of passage; all budding veterinarians must be reminded how much a cow weighs. No matter how strong you think you are, you are not stronger than a fifteen-hundred-pound cow.

When one veterinary student in the clinic learned we would be spending a day at a cattle ranch palpating cows, he was on cloud nine. Judging by his enthusiasm, I figured he had very little experience with ranches and cows. The forecast called for a high of 105 degrees with little to no wind. So, for about twelve hours, we'd be sticking our plastic-coated arms up the fannies of seven or eight hundred cows in the bottom of a boiling-hot canyon with no breeze.

My job was to palpate the cows for pregnancy and sort the open ones from the bred ones. The macho veterinary student was helping with the vaccinations and occasionally palpating. We had been at it for about five hours. The air was filled with dust that became plaster when it mixed with the continuous stream of sweat dripping from each of us. It was almost like rolling catfish in cornmeal after it had been coated with eggs and milk. And the temperature was nearly as hot as frying oil.

The big, muscled-up vet student was doing well. I'm guessing he could bench-press about three hundred pounds. I later concluded that this had given him a false sense of security.

Midway through our day, a one-eyed cow came barreling into the chute, slinging snot and high kicking with both back feet. I just love this kind of cow—they can only see what is happening on one side, so they are on a constant hunt for something sneaking up on them from the other side. You learn to get in and out of these wild ones in a hurry.

All of the cows at this particular ranch were a bit snakey, but this one-eyed girl was too much. I palpated her; thank goodness she was open. The cowboy hollered, "Open," and the student ran to the end of the alley to open the gate into the cull pen.

He just stood there on her blind side as she went by him. But he must have come into view of her good eye as she turned because she became a fifteen-hundred-pound veterinary student magnet. Her head went down, and snot started flying.

I guess my student hadn't seen that particular behavior in cows, because after you have seen a few of them go into the "I'm-gonna-pulverize-you" dance, climbing the nearest fence quickly becomes an involuntary response.

He made no attempt to scramble—he watched her head straight for him. I guess he figured she would stop and run away before she reached him. He was wrong! She made contact and started slinging him around like a rag doll.

I could see the thoughts running through his mind as she got her head under his fanny and effortlessly pitched him into the air. I could almost see the dialogue bubbles, as if he were a cartoon: "Bench-pressing three hundred pounds is meaningless, right?"

"I wish I didn't wear my pants so tight!"

"One-eyed cows are not afraid of veterinary students."

"Now I know why everyone scrambled for the fences!"

"I bet Dr. Brock will put this in his column."

We got to him just about the time she got tired of whoopin' on him. It was a pretty good pounding, judging from his torn-up britches and his bloodied nose. We got him in the pickup just in time to see him turn white and pass out.

I'm pretty sure he will never forget that day. He learned what the "I'm-gonna-pulverize-you" dance looks like. He learned that it's not sissy to climb a fence. He learned how to finish working cattle in a nearly nonexistent pair of britches. And, most of all, he learned that no matter how strong you think you are, you are not stronger than a cow.

Ostrich

Have you ever had a close encounter with an ostrich? Do you have any idea how big those rascals really are?

The first time I saw one in the flesh was when I responded to a call from the owners of a seven-foot-tall, 350-pound female ostrich. The big ol' bird that had stepped on something and had a raging infection in her foot. Even with a bum foot, the owners couldn't catch her. Actually, they were frightened to death of their birds.

My assignment: enter the enclosure, wrestle down the giant creature, remove whatever might be stuck in her foot, give her a shot, treat the abscess—and do it all without help from the couple who owned her.

Oh, they were full of advice, but that was as far as it went. They were not about to touch anything.

Their constant stream of advice was the farthest thing from my mind as I sized up the situation.

As I peered into a chicken-wire fortress, I sized up the toes on that bird. The biggest one must have been seven inches long, with a rock-solid, razor-sharp toenail on the end. I deduced that I should be more afraid of the feet than the head.

Then I saw the drumsticks. To carry and defend a 350-pound body, you need big drumsticks. I guessed that this beast packed quite a kick.

Then I wondered, *which way does she kick? Does she strike backward like a horse or forward like a rooster?* I went with the latter theory and decided I would treat her like a big chicken.

I noticed that the big bird's boyfriend was with her in the three-acre compound. He was even bigger than she, standing at least eight feet tall.

When I entered the pen, much to my surprise, both ostriches just sidled on up to me and started pecking at anything shiny—first my ring and then the button on top of my cap. This gave me a chance to assess the foot injury at close range. It was bad.

I realized that there was no way I was going to be able to pick up that foot. Every time I tried to touch it, the bird let out a mighty hiss, opening her mouth so wide that her face disappeared.

I left the pen and headed for a cell phone. I had no idea how to sedate an ostrich but figured I must know someone who did. The guy on the phone had very little advice—just the appropriate dose of anesthetic, a chuckle, and a warning to "give the shot in the muscles of the breast."

Back in the enclosure, I quickly discovered that I couldn't chase down the ostrich, even with an abscessed foot. So, I had the inspired idea to hide behind a bush in a small gully, wait for her to come by, stick her with the injection, and wait for her to fall asleep.

Things were looking good.

The owners waved a food bowl outside the fence to attract the bird's attention. She saw it and headed that way, right toward my hiding spot. That's when I noticed that the gully was just deep enough that I wouldn't be at the right angle to reach the breast muscles.

By then, however, I was committed. I jumped out at her, reached under her left wing and gave the shot while my legs dangled off her right side. This bird was actually carrying me! No part of me was making contact with the ground, and that made me uncomfortable. I tumbled off and to a stop as the owners cheered me on.

That's when I saw *him*.

Oh yes, him. He was coming right for me. The once-docile male ostrich had become quite defensive of his girlfriend in her moment of distress. He spread his white-tipped wings and came at me brimming of bad intentions.

I took off. But, at the end of about ten running steps, I learned that you cannot climb chicken wire.

Things were getting desperate. There was no way I could outrun this guy, leaving me with nothing left to do but fight. I looked around for some sort of weapon—a stick, a rock, anything—with which to defend myself. Nothing.

I had no choice but to face him with only my hands to protect me.

Without even thinking, I just braced myself and started yelling at him.

"Hey, get outta here!" I screamed, as I waved my arms and kicked dirt.

That was all it took! He folded up and ran the other way as if he'd seen a ghost.

My heart was pounding, and I was shaking all over. All I could think as I hurried toward the gate and my freedom was, *Eight years of school for that?*

You'll be pleased to hear that the female ostrich responded well to treatment once we got the thorn out of her foot.

Those people didn't own ostriches much longer, as I recall.

As for me, I still have dreams about giant, white-winged birds chasing me around a chicken-wire pen I can't climb out of.

Motorcycles

This episode begins at 2:00 a.m. in an old Chevy pickup as I headed to sew up a horse. It was going to be another hour or so of driving, according to the directions I had received over the phone from the frantic woman.

Wonder why they couldn't get a vet a little closer than me to come out? I pondered. *No one else is stupid enough to answer the phone. Maybe all the vets in that area know these people, and there is something wrong with them. Man, is it cold. I won't get back home until four or five in the morning. . . .*

As I arrived at the address, I began to think that I must have written down the directions wrong. I was pulling into what appeared to be a junkyard. Car skeletons lined an area that was illuminated by one old streetlight.

I pulled in slowly between rows of silhouetted Harley motorcycles. Just as I was about to turn around and leave, a figure appeared out of the shadows of an old tin building.

He was a very large man, wearing a helmet with a metal spike coming out of the top, a pair of tattered jeans, and a leather vest. It must have been forty degrees outside, and this guy was wearing nothing but a leather vest. As he got closer, I could see that he was covered with tattoos. Before he reached the window of my pickup, more figures began to appear.

I was a little panicked. It was three o'clock in the morning, and I was in a junkyard with a motorcycle gang. What were the odds that these people had a horse? How was I going to explain to these folks why I had invaded their turf?

"You the vet doctor?" The first words that hit my ears came in a very gruff tone that seemed to echo off all the dead cars that surrounded us. "My horse got a bad cut on his belly. Come on in."

I couldn't believe it! These people actually had a horse! He pointed toward the tin barn and motioned for me to follow him. I pulled the truck closer and exited timidly with my vet bag. Inside were thirty or so leather-clad individuals and one cut-up horse. The room was totally silent as I entered. I could feel eyes inspecting me as I ambled over to examine the horse.

The spokesman for the group was the giant man's girlfriend, who was dressed just like he was. She began to explain to me how the horse cut himself, but I was so taken by the entire scene that I barely heard a word she said. The horse had a huge laceration that ran across just in front of his front legs. A large flap of skin about the size of a paper grocery sack hung down under the belly area. This was amazing, but it was nothing compared with the man who was holding the horse. He had on sunglasses and was wearing a pair of leather earmuffs that covered only one ear. On the top of the other ear, between his head and the sunglasses, was one of those two-sided razor blades like my dad used to shave with. This razor blade just stayed there, as though it was embedded in the top of his ear.

As if this scene were not surreal enough, I knew I was going to have to sedate this horse in order to suture its monstrous wound. What were these people going to do when they saw what this sedative did to the horse? I'm thinking fast, now. The last thing I wanted was to be mugged for my horse sedative. I could just imagine them experimenting with the effects of horse tranquilizers.

I pulled out the sedative and drew it into the 12-cc syringe. As I was filling it, the dude with the razor blade on his ear said, "Hey, doctor dude, whatcha got in the syringe?"

"This is Rompun. It's a horse tranquilizer," bubbled out of my lips in a high, pubescent voice.

"Cool. What'll it do to people?" he gruffed back at me.

"Well, due to the greater vascularity of the human brain, this stuff will almost always cause a stroke-like seizure if it is taken by people." That was probably the biggest line of bull I'd ever uttered.

"Harsh," was all he had to say.

Now, for the next problem. How was I going to fix this horse? I have felt pressure when fixing animals many times in my career, but never like this. I was pretty sure that these people were not going to accept anything less than a perfect horse when I finished.

It took me close to two hours to suture this rascal. I put more stitches in that horse than in any other animal in my career—not because it was the biggest cut I've ever sewed, but because I really didn't want to ever see these people again in my life.

After more than an hour of driving, two hours of sewing in a tin barn at a junkyard surrounded by people who looked like they needed to be in a Clint Eastwood movie—and all this done in near darkness—the tattooed lady handed me a sticky note with an address scribbled on it, while the giant man told me to send him a bill.

All I could think of was, *Fine with me. If I leave this place alive, I don't care if I ever get paid.*

About a month later, we got a letter in the mail. It was from the gang. They were just writing to tell me thanks for fixing the horse. He was doing great. They had taken out the stitches themselves (I guess with the razor blade on the horse holder's head), and they were very thankful that I had come out in the middle of the night. Also enclosed was a check for the full amount.

Five Pounds

After twenty-five years of giving public talks, there ain't too many situations I let myself get into that are going to be risky. There are just some crowds that I don't want to talk to and some places I just don't fit in. But, only six months after graduating from vet school, I hadn't figured this out yet.

I stood at a podium in front of about four hundred cattle raisers and proceeded to give a talk on injection-site lesions. Crap, I didn't know anything about them, but I had been asked to do it, and so I did. I had researched and studied enough that I thought I knew what to say. But man oh man, was I wrong and the crowd clearly sensed it. After I finished my talk, they peppered me with questions that were so difficult that Alex Trebek would have had no idea.

One man in particular was just wearing me out. I was about twenty-six, and he was about sixty. He could see that I had little experience, and he was really enjoying watching me sweat and stutter every time he asked a new question. Heck, I didn't know the answer to even one of his questions, and half of them had nothing at all to do with what I was there to talk about.

This went on and on. I couldn't believe that someone on the panel of "experts" hadn't already ended my section of the talk. They all just sat there with dumb looks on their faces and watched me get eaten alive. By the time the sixty-year-old got through with me, I was a babbling mess. I finally went back to my spot at the elongated table on the stage at the front of the room and vowed never to give a public talk again. There were four more panelists to go after me. This meant that I had to sit in front of this crowd and endure the glares from Mr. Sixty for at least another hour.

The next fella who spoke gave an incredibly boring talk about some random cattle-feeding principle. I didn't hear a word he said because my brain was still spinning from the thirty-minute interrogation. He finished and politely asked if there were any questions.

This was just what Sixty was waiting for. That rascal let loose on the boring speaker and asked him another round of stupid and meaningless questions that he couldn't answer either. Jeez, what a turdhead. I felt a little bit better for myself—at least I wasn't the only idiot on the panel, but I couldn't help feeling sorry for my fellow panelist because the latest questions were even more insulting and difficult.

This same scenario played out after the next two speakers took the podium. Ol' Sixty tore them up too. I was amazed at how rude this fella was, and my emotions had moved from insecurity to anger. He was just loving making a fool out of every person on that panel and, by now, he had become annoying to most of the people in the audience too.

Dave, a PhD researching IBR (infectious bovine rhinotracheitis) in feedlot cattle, was the last speaker. Dave was no neophyte to public speaking. He was a marvelous and quick-witted speaker. He was nearing sixty himself, and I detected no fear in his stride as he approached the podium to present the findings of his recent research.

Still, I felt a bit sorry for Dave even before any words came from his mouth. I knew Mr. Sixty was gonna pounce on anything that had to do with the already controversial subject of IBR. I didn't figure Dave would get a quarter of the way into his talk before he was interrupted with a know-it-all question from Sixty.

Dave began by introducing some facts about IBR and how his research trial had been designed. He has an expert way of using his voice to hold listeners' attention and a pleasant sense of humor that kept people interested, but I watched the expression on Mr. Sixty's face. Dave's great speaking style seemed to tick him off even more. I could tell that he was rapidly approaching his boiling point every time Dave offered another fact or finding. After watching Sixty through four speakers now, I determined his problem: He just couldn't stand it that *he* wasn't the center of attention, and at the moment Dave was stealing the show.

I was looking at the sixty-year-old heckler when Dave said that, during the trial, researchers had noticed three things about cattle that were infected with a field strain of IBR. They all ran a temperature of over 104 degrees, all went off feed for the first four days, and all lost five pounds.

Mr. Heckler's face twisted up as if he had just taken a bite of a lemon, and he leaped to his feet to holler out his pressing statement/question.

"Dr. Dave, I cannot believe that a man with your scientific background would even make a statement like that. Don't you know that a calf can lose five pounds just due to the stress of running through a squeeze chute?"

As I turned to Dave, I expected to see an expression similar to the one that had been on my face and those of Mr. Sixty's other three victims. But to my surprise, he was calm as a cucumber and began to reply almost as quickly as the last words had left Sixty's mouth.

"You are correct, sir!" Dave replied with a tone of complete confidence. "These were five-hundred-pound cattle that we were working with, and we ran one of them through the chute a hundred times, and he *disappeared!*"

Dave's joke resulted in complete and total laughter from the audience. I mean hard laughter. Not the kind that lasts for a couple of seconds and dissipates. No, the kind of belly laugh that wanes for a second, and then gets loud again in undulating waves that continue for minutes. I lead the laughter from the stage, and the other panelists were joining me at high volumes mixed with occasional knee slaps.

The expression on Mr. Sixty's face was the absolute best part of the moment. Words cannot describe the emotions that crossed that fella's mug as the entire crowd rejoiced at his expense. His skin tone went from a morbid whitish-gray to radish-red, highlighted with purple blossoms on his cheeks.

His eyebrows went from the very top of his forehead while he was spouting off the know-it-all question to shielding his eye sockets as the crowd laughed and pointed at him. His ears went back like those of a mad chestnut mare, not in heat and standing next to a stud with ideas she wasn't fond of.

Mr. Sixty's posture collapsed into a hunker, and he folded his arms on the table in front of him. He seemed to shrink from an incredibly large man to a fifth-grade boy who had just been sent to the principal's office. I could tell by his body language that we weren't gonna hear from Mr. Sixty again that day.

Dave finished his talk on IBR. It went superbly. I still remember some of his findings and use them in practice today. There was not another peep from the crowd, and the panel talk ended with a roundtable discussion that was productive and informative. As for ol' Sixty . . . not even a peep.

I went up to Dave after the thing had ended and told him that he was my hero. There is nothing I like better than a quick and clever wit. I will never forget that day and still consider Dave to be one of the coolest dudes I have ever met. I am not sure what happened to Sixty. I never saw or heard from him again. But I can guarantee you this: he learned his lesson that day about messing with Dave, the IBR man.

Broken Arm

"Useless as a one-armed paperhanger."

That's how my grandfather would describe me when I seemed to be all thumbs while trying to help with certain jobs.

Not long ago, the metaphor came true when a manic racehorse kicked my right hand and broke my thumb. "Useless" may be the best way to describe a right-handed veterinarian who can't use his right thumb. "Frustrated" is what I'd call it.

Though I didn't miss any surgeries or turn anyone away, having only four fingers on my right hand made everything take twice as long with my thumb, wrist, palm, and upper forearm encased tightly in a heavy, rigid cast.

As I drove to the last farm call of the day, I hoped the job wouldn't take long. I had already been on several emergency calls and I was ready to get home. But, the donkey owner told me the foal had its head and one leg out, but the other leg was still inside, and things had gone south.

I pulled up to find a miniature donkey standing in a muddy pen, just as the owner had described. What he hadn't mentioned was that the baby appeared to be as large as its mother. In fact, the poor girl looked like a donkey with two heads—one at each end—and each about the same size. I realized this call was going to take more than a few minutes.

I've known the owner, a senior gentleman, for years and consider him a good friend. But, truth be told, I was thinking that he probably wouldn't be much help as I tried to deliver this baby one-handed.

He held the lead rope with a regretful, worried look on his face. That was all he could do—hold the rope and offer words of encouragement as I struggled. And struggle I did. This thing was wearin' me out. I pulled, tugged, grunted, groaned, got pulled through the mud, stepped on, and rolled over as I tried to unstick that leg from the four-hundred-pound momma donkey using mostly my left hand.

After thirty minutes, the leg was in the exact place it had been when we started and I needed a break. I went back to my pickup truck to regroup. My left arm was cramping, and my cast was broken. My glasses were caked with afterbirth, and this donkey had dragged me around enough to fill my underwear and trousers with wet dirt and straw.

I hadn't had mud in the creases of my body since I visited the beach as a little kid. I didn't like it then, and I don't like it now. It squished around as I sat in the truck and called my wife to let her know I'd be home late.

Finally, during the thirty-minute second round, the leg popped out. I started celebrating as if I'd just won a gold medal. All I had to do now was pull the baby the rest of the way out, and everything would be fine.

Wrong.

It still wouldn't come out. The jenny had lain down, so when I pulled on the baby, she'd just scoot around the pen. I couldn't hold her and pull the baby at the same time, so I asked the owner if any neighbors were around who might give us a hand.

There were. About twenty minutes later, a man—like the owner, a bit past middle age—showed up to assist. We all tried for a while and decided we needed even more reinforcements. Soon the owner's grandson (about my age) arrived. That did it. Some pulled, and some held, and the baby finally came the rest of the way out.

The momma donkey did just fine but I was a mess. I had not been that dirty since childhood and my cast was ruined. One of the benefits of being a veterinarian is that a hot shower always washes off the guck and you can easily make yourself a new cast when the old one breaks.

Blue Minivan

I think every veterinarian should take the time to write down proper directions. If I were in charge of veterinary school curriculum, I would make Rural Navigation and Communications a required class for senior veterinary students.

Since becoming a veterinarian, I have been lost countless times. The problem usually lies in one overwhelming fact: The people who are giving the directions have lived in the area in question for years, and the person getting the directions has not. Every region has its own set of navigational terms that you must learn in order to interpret client directions.

Over the years, I have learned that the secret lies in a few key "do nots":

1. **Do not** write down any direction that has the word "before" in it. Here is an example: "You will turn left about a mile and a half before you get to an S-shaped curve in the road." Sounds crazy, but it has happened to me two or three times since I have started taking directions. You would think that I would have learned after the first mile-and-a-half trip back that "before" invariably means you'll have to backtrack. How is that helpful?

2. **Do not** write down any direction that has time as a unit of measure. Here is an example: The seventy-five-year-old rancher who comes to town only every other Monday tells you, "And then you'll go straight on that road for about ten minutes and turn back to the east." How far do you think that fella went in ten minutes? Three miles, four miles? At a mile a minute, it would be ten miles. Never in a hundred years would I have guessed it was one mile, but it was. That is right, he drives one mile in ten minutes. Wow! No wonder he comes to town only twice a month.

3. **Do not** write down any directions that have "relative" terms. Here is an example: "You will be on a paved road now. Stay on this road until you come to a dirt road with deep ditches. You will turn south there." I had to go back and forth on that road for what seemed like hours comparing the depth of ditches until I determined which one appeared to be the deepest. I was figuring when I wrote the directions down that there would be one dirt road with deep ditches. Wrong. They all had deep ditches. This guy only noticed the one he always drives on.

4. **Do not** write down any landmark that is not fixed to the earth. Here is an example: "After you turn here, you will go awhile until you come to a house with a blue minivan parked in the driveway. You will make a right there." Of course, the minivan was gone when I happened by. I drove about ten miles past the intended house before I finally gave up and went back.

There are a few other things worth mentioning. The only way that a place can be named after a person is if they are dead or have moved away. This further complicates learning an area for a newcomer. Here is an example: "You will drive south on this road until you come to the edge of the old Carlton place. You will turn east here." Come to find out that Mr. Carlton died in 1944 and has no living relatives.

Another thing worth mentioning is volume. If the directions have a repetition of more than five things in them as you encounter the landmark, jot a mark on your windshield. Here is an example: "After this, you will be on the ranch. You will go straight for quite a while, and then you will veer left after the twelfth cattle guard." Of course, you know that I lost count at seven and had to go back and start all over.

By far, the most important thing to do is get specifics. Things like barn color, house color, building materials used, county road numbers, exact measurements, mailboxes, telephone poles, and any natural landmarks will cut down on how much fun it is to drive aimlessly through the countryside for half a day comparing ditch depth.

I've become so intent on getting good directions that I'm sure I get on some people's nerves. For example, I made one man describe every detail about his house and its surroundings, only to find when I got there that it was the only house for miles.

Cauliflower

I arrived a bit late at the continuing-education meeting and stood at the door, trying to decide where to sit. After a busy workday, it's hard to make these evening meetings on time, especially when they're sixty miles away.

The crowd was already seated around tables, waiting for dinner to be served. I didn't know anyone, so I just chose the first open seat I came to, introduced myself to those at the table, and began evaluating them subconsciously, as we all are prone to do.

The meeting topic had attracted both city and rural veterinarians. I always enjoy these kinds of meetings because they bring together the wide variety of people and personalities who make up our profession.

The circular table seated twelve. To my left was a group from a rural veterinary practice—a vet and four techs, still wearing a bit of the day's aroma. To my right was another DVM, his wife, and four techs who obviously had spent their day inside, working on small animals.

Conversation was minimal. Groups like this have little in common and often sit on different sides of the veterinary fence.

The city-vet's wife seemed a bit abrasive. She was considerably overdressed for the occasion and seemed to look down her nose at the country vets. As luck would have it, she was immediately to my right; I, too, was a bit smelly after a long, hot day.

The arrival of dinner seemed to cut the tension a bit. We were served a chicken dish with steamed vegetables. The veggies would have been good if cooked properly, but these were a bit rubbery. There was broccoli, cauliflower, squash, and some other green thing that I couldn't identify.

The servers came by to pour a glass of wine for those who wanted it. Most of us declined, but the ritzy wife asked them to leave the whole bottle. It didn't take her long to consume it, with only a little help from her husband and a younger woman. The more the wife drank, the ruder she became. She went on about how great their clinic was and how smart her husband was.

Then she began praising the quality of the food as she chomped down on those steamed veggies. As I looked around the table, no one else had been able to cut even one piece into a bite small enough to eat.

The young woman to my left, from the country practice, seemed a bit shy. Her hands told a story of hard work, and she was not digging those vegetables. I watched her work on the cauliflower. It was so large and perfectly round that she couldn't figure a way to cut it. She tried the fork first. No luck. Then she tried stabbing it with the fork. Again, no luck. Finally, she held it with the fork and cut it with the knife.

This led to a remarkable event: when she pressed down with the knife, the rubbery cauliflower suddenly shot off her plate, bounced once in my lap, and came to rest somewhere deep within the ritzy wife's partly opened purse.

We just looked at each other with one-cornered smiles and kept listening to the now semidrunk, overdressed woman go on about something that she thought made her look great and the rest of us look stupid. We never said a word.

That cauliflower was drenched in some high-viscosity sauce that left a stain on my trousers. I could just imagine what it must be doing to the contents of that high-dollar purse. As I started to say something about it, she looked at me and made some subliminally rude comment about my practice. I just smiled and nodded.

I wonder where she was when she found that cauliflower. I laughed about it all the way home. She left the room that night with a baseball-sized piece of cauliflower and would most likely blame me for it at some point.

Oh well.

Cop and Reindeer

The roads of West Texas are painfully lonely at 2:00 a.m. In fact, I had not seen a car in twenty minutes as I sped toward a waiting reindeer.

Why does it seem that reindeer always go into labor at 2:00 a.m.?

There is one thing about being the only vehicle on the road—you are very noticeable. As I mounted the only hill in Gaines County, there was nothing else for the police officer to see except a speeding veterinarian headed for a reindeer delivery.

Great. There is no way this guy is going to believe me, I thought as he pulled me over.

He ambled up to the truck with that typical "cautious policeman" gait. I could feel the beam of his flashlight bouncing off of my head as I anticipated his smirk when I informed him of my mission.

"Could I see your driver's license, please, sir?"

"Well, Mr. Brock, any reason you are in such a hurry at this late hour?"

I always feel like a third-grader who has been sent to the principal's office when the law pulls me over. As much as I wanted to sound convincing, I just choked up on the next few words that came out of my mouth. The noise that poured forth sounded like a fourteen-year-old boy who was going through the "yodel" that comes with puberty.

"Um, yes, Officer, I was just on my way to deliver a reindeer baby."

If I had not been in such a hurry, the look that came over his face would have been something to savor. But with the urgency of the matter, I decided to expound a bit more.

"You see, I am a veterinarian, and there is a female reindeer about five miles down the road that is having a critical time delivering; she's having a dystocia."

I decided to throw in the big word there at the end to perhaps add a bit of credibility to my claim. It was not until this moment in my veterinary history that I realized that there was no way to prove that I actually am a veterinarian!

"You mean to tell me that you are speeding through the warm, West Texas night to deliver a baby reindeer? Well, I've heard it all now," came bubbling from his lips behind an expression that joined a slight grin with a look of disgust.

"Listen, my friend, this reindeer is worth about ten thousand bucks if I can get it out before it dies. I know you are here to enforce the law, so if you are going to give me a ticket, would you mind following me over to the reindeer and writing it out as I bring that critter into the world?"

My pubescent voice had turned to an incredibly authoritative one with absolutely no conscious effort. In fact, I was hoping that I had not sounded too bossy when some bass finally came back to my tones.

Much to my surprise, the officer suddenly became excited and urgent himself. He almost panicked. He began shuffling his feet and folding the papers in his hands. He looked down the road as if to visualize this reindeer going through the Lamaze steps in anticipation of her doctor arriving.

"I just don't believe anyone could make something like that up," he said. "You just run along now and save that baby's life."

"Good luck," was the last thing I heard him say as I pulled back onto the road.

I got there in plenty of time to help li'l Rudolph take his first breath. I've often wondered if the police officer went back to the station and told his buddies, or if he just kept it to himself, figuring they would all make fun of him and think he was crazy.

I've also wondered if it will work the next time I get pulled over.

Tough Crowd

It occurred to me one day, as I spoke to a client, that my job often requires telling folks things they don't want to hear—bad news about a disease, tough love about diets for fat pets, problems that we have no cure for, or prices for procedures that may exceed their budgets. The list goes on and on. To top it off, I really never know how they will take the news or what their response may be.

A friend had asked me to give a funny talk to a group on a date near Christmas. I owed this woman a favor and said I'd be glad to give a talk. I have been blessed beyond what I deserve in many areas of life. I have given funny, motivational, and informative talks all over this country and overseas. I remember many of them with fondness and smiles. On this occasion, I failed to ask who would be in this group. I wrote the date on my calendar and promptly forgot all about it. As the week of the talk approached, my friend called to remind me and give me the location.

I was surprised that the building was next to a hospital and that it didn't appear to be a meeting hall. I walked into a reception area and told the receptionist that I had been given directions to this location to give a talk. She smiled graciously and shook my hand. She led me through a series of hallways into an office, where I was instructed to wait, my friend would soon arrive.

I had my computer containing all of the usual funny animal slides. I was running through the talk in my head as my friend walked into the office. She gave me a big hug and thanked me profusely for coming to talk to her group. She said they sure needed a lift and something to laugh about during the holidays.

My curiosity began to rise when she said they sure needed a lift around the holidays. I thanked her for inviting me and then asked, tentatively, "Who, exactly, am I talking to?"

"You mean you don't know?" she asked, her eyebrows arched high on her forehead.

I was beginning to run through scenarios, wondering why I didn't know something that seemed so obvious to her. I was beginning to feel a little pressure and wasn't sure why.

"These people are all terminally ill. I have heard you give talks many times and think you will make them laugh and bring them happiness."

What? How did I miss this detail? My brain suddenly became mush as I considered the task. What in the world could I possibly say to dying people at Christmas that could make them happy? I very seldom find myself terrified of the audience before me. But on one particular occasion, I was terrified.

"I had absolutely no idea this would be the audience! I am not even kinda prepared to do this. I was just gonna give a talk about the life of a veterinarian and all the funny things we see every day. These people ain't gonna want to hear that stuff!"

The pitch of my voice and the sweat forming on my face clued her in to my panic. "Don't worry. I have heard that talk before. They will love it," she said in a calm tone that made me want to strangle her.

She led me down yet another hall, through a large double door, and into a conference room with nearly 150 hospital beds and soft chairs in it. The audience fit the bill of exactly whom she said I would be addressing.

She seated me on a stage next to a podium, and before I even had a moment to convince myself that everything would be OK, an A/V dude had my computer hooked up, and she finished her introductions.

I stood up behind that podium and looked out over the crowd. Those folks did not look like they were in any mood to laugh. Do you know how hard it is to tell stories that are supposed to be funny to people who don't laugh? It is awful. I had maybe fifteen stories to get through, and I was filled with dread. I could feel cold sweat dripping from every sweat-producing gland on my body. I must have stood there for a good fifteen seconds without uttering a word.

Finally, I found the courage to begin. Some lower level of my brain must have convinced an upper level of my brain that my talk would never be over if I didn't get started.

I went through the first story, laying it out with all the gusto I could muster. When I reached the point of the story that should invoke laughter, I heard not a peep.

It was my best story. If they didn't laugh at that, I might as well just get off that stage and head back to Lamesa. I was petrified. Five seconds, ten seconds, fifteen seconds and still there was not even a peep.

Just about the time I was ready to pack it in, an old dude in a wheelchair to my left began to cackle in a gruff, raspy roll. This prompted a woman in the fourth row, lying in a bed and wearing one of those hospital gowns that make you feel more naked than if you were actually naked, to start laughing loud and hard. The giggles spread, and soon the entire room was rumbling with leg-slapping belly-laughs.

I couldn't believe it. They were cracking up. Tears were running down faces that looked as though they hadn't smiled in years. I paused for a long moment to absorb what had just happened. My story is pretty funny, but it had never made anyone laugh like that.

I talked for about two hours. We had the best time. I went out into the audience as I spoke and got them involved in the stories. They thanked me a thousand times for coming, and I must have gotten a sloppy cheek kiss from half the audience.

As I was talking to that client, I remembered that evening with the people I thought would never laugh. You just never know by looking who might be dying for a reason to smile.

Six

Cowboys, Old Men, and Oddballs

I will never say that I, myself, am a cowboy, but I idolized cowboys in my youth. They are still amazing to me. They possess the perspective that I find to be the most interesting.

Perhaps I define a cowboy a little differently than Hollywood. These are men who work outside raising crops and livestock. They are the most creative and intelligent people I know. Just consider what cowboys have accomplished over the last hundred or so years: tractors that can pull giant plows and manage abundant crops and cattle that can thrive and become the beef that nourishes us. If you have ever been around cowboys, you will understand that they have a way of doing things that is unlike any other.

Most of them can repair or manufacture just about anything that is needed to keep a ranch running. They can weld and build with wood. They can string fence for miles. They can deliver calves and keep horses sound. They can stand the hottest and coldest conditions Mother Nature has to offer. They seldom complain and have a perspective on nature that often goes untold.

I have had the good fortune of knowing cowboys. I have spent countless hours in their company learning how to live off the land and respect nature, with all of its beauty and wrath.

I am becoming an old man. I feel certain that some young veterinarian will be writing some words years from now about old men, and I will be mentioned. I have come to accept that old is gonna happen no matter what I do to try to stop it. My eyebrows are gonna get coarse and long, my belly button is gonna get deeper, and my hair is gonna get sparse and white. With all of those changes come a touch of wisdom, but probably not as much as I'd like.

Kidney

Sometimes it's good for the doctor to be the one being doctored. It's a small reminder of what those critters are going through while we try to get them well. I had an event a few years ago that really tuned me in to pain and treatments.

I was watching a football game and waiting for church time to come around, when suddenly it felt like someone sneaked into my room and kicked me in the stomach. The primitive part of my brain processed, *Sharp pain in the midgut area, Bo,* while the logic part of my brain theorized, *No one could have snuck in here and kicked me in the stomach without me seeing him.*

I figured it would pass in a second. But the pain just kept building and building and I was starting to curl up. Pretty soon, my knees were nearing my chin. What was happening? I remembered those classes we took while Kerri was pregnant. *In through your mouth, out through your nose,* I thought. *Hoo-hoo-heehoo-hoo-hee.* It didn't help.

Here it was late December, and I was dripping sweat. I thought about horses with colic, and how they just drip with sweat when their pain intensifies. But "intense" was an understatement: I was lying in a puddle on the floor when Kerri came in to ask me if I was ready for church.

Church? Are you kidding? I'm not sure I can stand. A mere ten minutes had passed since the phantom kicker had sneaked into the room, but I felt as though I had been hunched over for hours.

"What's the matter with you?" she asked with concern in her eyes.

I blathered something about a steel-toe-boot-wearing phantom who just had his way with me.

We substituted the hospital for church. I had no idea what was happening, but I knew that if I didn't get some relief soon, I was going to dehydrate from sweating.

The woman at the front desk must have seen this hunkered-over stance before: bent over at the waist, hands curled around the midsection, profuse sweating accompanied by a mild moan with each exhale.

"Passing a kidney stone, I see," she said matter-of-factly.

Is that what is happening to me? I'd heard about kidney stones, and I knew things were going to get worse before they got better.

They sent me home with pain medicine and a paper cup in which to catch the rascal. *This thing must be as big as a grapefruit,* I thought. *I'm gonna catch it and have it bronzed—preserve it for posterity.*

The pain medicine kept me a bit stoned all night, so I didn't really look in the cup at the end of each trip to the bathroom. The folk at the hospital had given me some fluids, so I must have made five or six visits throughout the night.

I felt much better when morning broke. That thing must have passed, and I knew I would find it in that paper cup in the bathroom. I couldn't wait to see the offending grapefruit. I snatched up the paper cup, and there it was: huge and brown with spikes all over it. No wonder it hurt so bad.

"Kerri, come have a look at this beast," I called. "It must be the granddaddy of all kidney stones."

"That's not a kidney stone," she said with a confused look on her face.

Upon further examination, it seemed that some poor bug had wandered into the cup at some point in the night, and I had blown it to pieces, leaving just one leg attached to its body. The real stone was there, too. At the very bottom of the cup, and not much bigger than a comma.

"A comma?" That little thing caused all this? I'd need to rethink my bronzing idea.

I often remember being doubled over in pain from the kidney stone as I doctor critters. I now have a much better idea of what it's like to have a surprise visit from the pain phantom and to have no idea what is going on when you go see the doctor.

Jimmy Stewart

I guess one of my favorite things about being a veterinarian is helping to bring a new critter into the world.

After more than ten years and thousands of deliveries, it still stirs a special sentiment within me.

It was an average afternoon when the phone rang. A local rancher's heifer was having trouble calving. I'd been in Clarendon long enough to know most of the people who have livestock in the area, and I knew how they liked to do things. When this fellow called to tell me he couldn't get the calf out himself, I knew this call was going to be a doozy.

I headed out to lend a hand. The rancher reminded me of Jimmy Stewart. He had the same sound to his voice and moved his head and neck like the actor. The similarities made it a lot of fun to be around him, even with the poor calf presenting upside down and twisted.

We got this heifer into the chute and started the tedious process of straightening out the calf. For those of you who have not had the privilege of trying to pull a seventy-five-pound calf out of a narrow-hipped heifer, I offer a couple of analogies: It is sorta like doing a carburetor job through the tailpipe, or pulling a marshmallow out of a piggy bank. I had been laboring—along with the heifer—for about thirty minutes when I got a total body cramp and had to take a breather.

Upon seeing this, Jimmy Stewart hopped in and spelled me. He pulled and twisted, moaned and sputtered, and finally tagged off to me again. By now, the heifer had lain down and was not even attempting to push.

We were both covered in that sticky cow juice that accompanies a birth. It's like God's WD-40, and boy, is it slick! In fact, if you step in it in an unfocused moment, you will surely slide as if you are skating on ice, flinging your arms to balance.

Over the years, I have developed the ability to wrestle a stuck calf while talking on the phone, answering questions from other clients, and lining up appointments. Most of the time at the vet clinic, someone is sure to be standing around spectating and commentating like Cliff Clavin—they have seen it all and done it all.

This day was no exception. Some fellow I had not seen before and haven't seen since showed up and started offering his two cents. I just go on about my business when there's a spectator, but Jimmy Stewart, on the other hand, was used to doing this without an audience, and his nerves were fraying.

It was Jimmy's turn with the calf when this guy walked up. He was engulfed in one of those heavy straining moments when Cliff Clavin offered, "I had an aunt who could just walk out into the field and pull one of those things out."

Now, I have heard those kinds of tales since my first day as a vet. The anecdote bounced right off me. I just figured this spectator had no idea what he was talking about, and he couldn't keep his ignorance to himself. I had no idea that Jimmy was paying any attention at all when, just about the time he got the calf untwisted, he lost his grip, and the calf recoiled to the very position it was in when we started about an hour earlier.

Frustration had reached an all-time high. I told him to take a break and let me have another shot.

The spectator started in again. This time he said, "She could have really done good if she would have had one of these fancy things to catch the cow in."

The comment bounced off again. But much to my surprise, when I looked up at the normally mild-mannered Jimmy, his face had turned beet red, and I'm sure I saw a puff of smoke coming out of each ear.

"It's not that easy, you see," he said in a perfect Stewart accent. "This calf is all twisted up, you see."

If you can imagine Jimmy Stewart in *It's a Wonderful Life*, you'll have a great sense of just exactly how this guy looked.

"If she is so good at this, why don't you just go and get her?" he finally said.

Upon hearing this, the spectator turned and left. I don't know if I was just simpled out or if Jimmy's comment was really that funny, but I got to laughing so hard that I had to quit pulling on that calf and just lie there in the cow juice. I was laughing so hard I wasn't even making any noise.

Jimmy apologized to me: "I hope I didn't run off one of your clients."

I told him not to worry.

We finally got the calf out and went on with life. I often think about that moment, Jimmy standing there, covered in the slickest, slipperiest substance in the world—it was even in his hair, making it stick straight up—red-faced, sleeves rolled up, frustrated beyond words, telling the spectator to just go and get that aunt, who, by the way, never showed up.

Mr. Ford

We prefer to do surgery in the morning—my favorite time of day—before the telephone starts ringing and emergencies begin showing up. It's peaceful, and surgery usually can be done without hurry or distraction.

Some of the townsfolk like to hang out at our clinic, perhaps while a flat is getting fixed or rain has stopped their work for a while. One older gentleman, Mr. Ford, stopped by regularly to watch surgery, even though we often begin as early as 6:00 a.m.

This particular morning was chilly, so Manda stoked up our little gas heater to add some warmth to the surgery room. The thing fits on top of a propane bottle and gets red-hot.

Mr. Ford was there, storytelling as usual. We'd heard most of his stories many times. If someone came in with a horse, he might tell the one about the prize racehorse he ran in 1955 (pretty sure I've heard that one a thousand times). Some people would walk away, but others would listen for thirty minutes or more. He loved it. It was what he lived for. I never complained. It gave clients something to do while they waited, and it made him happy.

That morning, he was standing in front of the red-hot heater, talking about how smart his dog was. Being familiar with that one, too, most of us had tuned him out for the moment as we fished around for a bone chip in a horse's knee.

I'm not sure who smelled it first, but we all looked up at the same time.

Something was burning.

About that time, Mr. Ford, in a calm and casual voice, said, "I'm on fire."

He had backed into the heater until his britches touched the hot grill and began to burn. Smoke was coming from just above the bend of his knee, but he was patting himself on the back pockets, trying to put it out. At eighty-four years of age, bending down that low is perhaps more painful than being on fire.

Everyone in the room went into fire mode. Manda started beating the burning pants with a towel, but that just seemed to stoke the flames and create more smoke. The fire grew worse as others in the room looked around for something to put it out. I was thinking of throwing Mr. Ford on the ground and rolling him around, but decided that might hurt him. Besides, I was sterile for the surgery. We needed water, but there was none to be found—unless we picked him up and put him in the sink.

Then it hit me.

I pulled the arthroscope out of the cannula and aimed it at Mr. Ford's leg. Manda saw it happening and turned up the pressure on the pump to high. The lavage fluid hit the burning pants, and in seconds, the fire was out. I didn't even break sterility!

It was all just a blip to Mr. Ford, who, calm as a cucumber, resumed his story exactly where he had left off.

Mr. Ford passed away a few months back. We miss him and his interesting tales. But what we'll remember most is that chilly morning when his trousers caught fire.

I can't help but wonder how many surgeons can say they've extinguished a burning pair of pants with an arthroscope and never broken sterility?

Tex

We had three horses with serious colic, a pig under anesthesia, a cow with a prolapse that was trying to birth a calf, and a waiting room full of dogs. In times like these you can't decide what to do first, and everyone needs you "right this minute." But none of them needed us more than Tex.

Tex stood patiently with his horse while he waited his turn. The horse was very sick, and it appeared as if we were going to have to do a colic surgery. The anesthetized pig was on the surgery table with its nose covered by an oxygen mask, and the cow was in the chute, straining and grunting to no avail.

I had gone into the clinic to get instruments to do the pig surgery, when my ear caught that spine-tingling sound of someone gagging as though he might throw up. With all the nasty smells that a veterinary clinic can produce, we heard this sound on occasion. But when I looked back out the door into the large-animal waiting room, I saw ol' Tex, just piled up in the corner in a position that any normal fifty-five-year-old had avoided for at least forty-five years. It was as if he was sitting down, but both of his feet were higher than his head. This caused me some concern.

Dr. Zach Smith was looking at me as I looked out the door. He had heard the retching, but he couldn't see through the doorway. He must have detected the panic on my face, because we both ran at the same time.

Tex was trying to get his feet from behind his head when we approached. I wasn't sure what had happened, but I knew it was going to take some doing to get him out of the knot he had fallen into. Zach pulled one way, and I pulled the other. With a few tugs, Tex uncoiled and got to his feet.

"I just gotta get a little air," he muttered as he headed for the garage door.

We followed him with great concern as he bent over the tailgate of a pickup. I was a bit worried, and the expression on Zach's face was no consolation, either.

"You gonna be all right?" Zach asked.

"Just need a little air is all," Tex muttered.

"Why don't we take you inside and let you lay on the couch for a minute?" Zach persisted.

To my surprise, Tex agreed.

You know something must be terribly wrong when a tough ol'

cowboy dude says he'll go inside and lie down. Zach and I each took a side, but about three steps into the journey, Tex collapsed. Zach caught him, and we carried him over to the horse-surgery table.

Now we had an anesthetized pig on the pig-surgery table, Tex's horse rolling around in pain on the floor of the surgery room, Tex passed out on the horse-surgery table not two feet from the sleeping pig, and two docs without a clue as to what to do next.

I remember thinking that Tex would get pretty good care if he were a pig or a horse. We went to work.

Zach felt for a pulse in his wrist, and I listened to his chest with a stethoscope. Neither of us found a thing.

"Oh my, oh my, oh my," I stammered as I grabbed the pulse oximeter off the pig's tongue and hooked it to Tex. It read a heart rate of 180 and a blood-oxygen count of seventy-six; humans need ninety-five.

Zach stayed fairly composed, but I panicked. I grabbed the oxygen mask off the pig and put it on Tex. I started moving toward his chest; I figured if there was any CPR fixin' to happen, Zach could do the mouth-to-mouth part, and I would do chest compressions.

"You'd better call the ambulance, Bo," Zach said.

I'd be willing to wager that it was the first time an ambulance driver rolled onto a scene where two veterinarians were using pig techniques on a cowboy having a heart attack. We had him hooked to monitors, and we were giving him oxygen through the pig mask. We were listening to his chest and trying to check eye responses.

In our combined fifteen years of veterinary experience, we had treated at least a hundred crashing animals, but we were overwhelmed with the prospect of losing one human life.

———

Everything turned out OK. Tex went to the Lamesa Hospital, where they fixed him up and had him back at the clinic in about four hours to see his horse. His ticker was fine; he was hypoglycemic.

I just talked to him the other day, in fact, and he said the only side effects from the entire ordeal are a faint oink when he coughs and a subconscious urge to root around in the dirt of the backyard.

Mr. Teeth

Vets always seem to keep an eye on teeth. Many of our patients would like to sink them into us. Today, though, the teeth we were watching out for were a bit unusual.

Dr. Zach Smith was knee-deep in stink. The mare was pregnant, but the baby had died inside of her several days before she arrived at the clinic and was beginning to decompose. This makes for a smell that you just can't know until you've experienced it. The fly population was having a heyday. They were everywhere and seeming to multiply on contact.

As is usually the case in our office, several people were standing around watching and willing to lend a helping hand. But delivering a dead foal is a slow and tortuous job and the crowd started thinning as the really smelly parts started coming out. Only the dedicated and brave at heart remained. One gentleman in particular was determined not to let Zach go it alone. He was gloved up and bouncing from place to place like a puppy dog around the table, just waiting for his chance to jump in and help.

The parts became bigger and bigger until finally the torso started its journey out. The smell became overwhelming. It was at about this time that the gentleman got a nose full of the wretched stink. This is one of those smells that is so bad that you can perceive it with senses other than just your nose. It seems to get into your eyes, the pores of your skin, and the hair in your nostrils, and it even has a taste. It was noticeable that Mr. Teeth's senses were inundated as the large part of the foal came sliding out.

Turns out this fellow had just gotten false teeth. I guess the smell had saturated the new chompers, too. Whatever the case, it started some of those gut-busting heaves. They started slow and silent. Then they rolled into longer, louder contractions of the chest and stomach. All attention left the horse and went to Mr. Teeth.

"He's gonna blow! Run away!" yelled Zach as the crowd started backing away.

Mr. Teeth was making all kinds of guttural noises now. His cheeks would puff out like Louis Armstrong's, only to be followed by a deep blowing sound as his dry lips succumbed to the building pressure of each dry heave. He was running around in circles, looking for a place to erupt. The situation was further complicated by the nasty gloves he was wearing. Each time he would reach toward his face to quiet the swells, the goo that was on the gloves would increase the intensity of the smell.

People were scattering like buckshot, but they all wanted to stay close enough to see what happened next.

Zach started barking orders. "Puke in the sawdust! Don't run that way; there's nothing to vomit on! Go outside! Take your gloves off!"

None of the words seemed to penetrate the prevomit fog that had overtaken Mr. Teeth. He just kept running in circles and touching his face with the slimy gloves. It seemed like it was going to go on forever.

It was on about his thirtieth lap that the sound of those teeth chattering became the dominant noise. They were bumping into his lips, his gums, and each other. It sounded a bit like somebody rolling dice in a Yahtzee cup. It was obvious that everyone would need to duck when those babies came flying out. It was just a question of which way they were going to go; as he would spin, the audience would bend and rise at the waist like football fans doing the Wave.

Finally, the teeth were airborne. There had been enough pressure built up to propel them at a rapid rate. Mr. Teeth had managed to slip behind the surgery room, into an area that afforded a safe launch. No one actually saw it happen, but we all heard the impact. The noise was something similar to a car backfiring, followed by a high-pitched ping as the teeth flew out of his mouth and bounced off a metal I-beam.

Ghastly looks were immediately replaced by raised eyebrows and gut-busting laughter. After finishing the job, Mr. Teeth calmly went over, picked up his new teeth, and put them right back in his mouth. What a day!

First C-section

I was watching our oldest daughter, Emili, handle the wheel as she steered the car for the first time. We've always made driving look so easy, she probably assumed it was a snap. I had to move the wheel several times to keep us from hitting mailboxes and swerving into a ditch. After a few practice runs and some nervous moments, I'm sure she'll be fine. In a few more years, she'll be driving while talking on the phone, drinking a soda, and changing the radio station, all at the same time. Her certain evolution in confidence reminded me of my first C-section on a cow.

I was three weeks post graduation, surrounded by cowboys who had seen many more C-sections than I had. In fact, I had never seen even one. This meant that the first one I was going to see was also the first one I was going to do. Think about that, and then get nervous with me.

To make matters worse, these weren't just any cowboys. They were from a ranch that had a reputation for being the best around. I was irked at my veterinary school for never in four years affording me the opportunity to see or practice this procedure, although I did see it once on film.

The cowboys sized me up, knowing that I was new in town. They watched my every move, peering right through my artificial confidence. I was already half exhausted from trying to deliver the calf. I had pulled, poked, strained, twisted, lubricated, sweated, and groaned for about two hours. All the other veterinarians were gone, and there was no one to turn to except these fifteen guys, all of whom looked like the Marlboro Man. And—no pressure—they all thought I knew what I was doing.

The vet-school film I had seen showed the calf being delivered from the underside, with the cow on her back. I gathered from the cowboys that Dr. Deyhle performed C-sections through the left flank, with the cow standing.

What was I going to do? I'd never even seen a cow cut open in the flank, much less delivered a calf through that area. On the other hand, if they'd never seen one taken through the belly, they wouldn't know if I was messing up. Using that logic, I told them recent research had shown that the calf and cow did much better if the baby was taken through the belly, and, with no visible scar, cows usually sold better. This produced some low murmurs of agreement as they pondered the new idea.

If there's one thing I've learned about people who live fifty miles from the nearest town, it is that any new idea must be considered for awhile before it is accepted.

After some high-level discussion among the oldest cowboys, it was decided the belly approach would be OK. We already knew that the calf had died. Apparently, they decided there wasn't much to lose.

They let the cow out of the chute, jumped on her, and in no time had her tied up and lying on her back. The stage was all mine. With trembling hands, I went to work. We put a local block in her belly, and I went to cutting. As sheer dumb luck would have it, the surgery went perfectly. I was in and out of that cow in about twenty minutes. She got up and went into the trailer as if nothing had ever happened.

The guys thought they'd just witnessed the newest thing in C-sections. As they drove off, I could hear them talking about the benefits of the "belly approach," and how great it was that there was no scar that would keep her from selling.

As for me, I was never so glad to be finished with anything in my life. I could feel my stomach acid churning away at the ulcer I was surely growing. How many more of these "first-time-see-and-do" procedures would I have to endure?

I finally got to see Dr. Deyhle do one with the cow standing. Boy, is it easier! I never did another C-section through the belly of a cow for anyone but those ranchers and, if I can help it, I never will. However, the veterinarian who does most of their work today tells me those cowboys insist that every C-section be done through the belly. I guess we all have to nearly hit the mailbox and swerve a few times before we gain confidence.

I've done hundreds of C-sections over the years now. I can do them even while talking on the phone, drinking a soda, and changing the radio station.

GI Joe

Everyone calls him Pink. I have no idea what his real name is; he's just always been Pink to me. He comes into the clinic with his Chihuahuas, and as long as I have been in Lamesa, we have been friends.

He must be around eighty-five now, though it seemed like he was that old twenty years ago when I came to Lamesa. He is just one of those fellas who must have been born looking eighty-five and never got any older. He has an opinion about everything and is not afraid to express it.

When he comes to the clinic, he stays for hours. He will just sit in the waiting room with one of his five or six dogs and talk to everyone who comes in. He has stories about the war (not sure if he was actually in one or just heard about it), stories about farming cotton (he never farmed in his life), stories about police work (he has a grandson who is a policeman), and stories about all the smart things his dogs can do (they are absolutely not smart).

This particular day found a group of local farmers gathered in the lobby of the clinic looking at a dog that had gotten into paraquat, a defoliant that the farmers around here use. This great big dog had somehow managed to get into it big-time. They had carried that thing into the lobby and just set it on the floor right in the middle of the room.

Pink was there with his favorite Chihuahua, Monster, tucked under his left arm. He was going on about how paraquat was like the Agent Orange they had sprayed in Vietnam. He went on and on about all the nasty effects and how it had killed billions of soldiers.

I was examining the dog and listening to all the country folk go over the vast amount of trivial knowledge they seemed to keep stored up in their brains—this time, about defoliants. I really couldn't remember everything I needed to know about paraquat, so I announced that I was going to my office to get Dr. Bailey's notes from vet school.

These guys remind me of Cliff Clavin on *Cheers*. They know everything about everything and seem to want nothing more than to top each other with another level of smarts (I call it BS) just as soon as there is a momentary pause in conversation. I had heard about all I could stand, and going for the notes seemed like a good way to collect my thoughts in peace and not have to listen to them endlessly one-upping each other with war stories and farming practices.

Pink was leading the BS competition by a large margin when I left for the office. He was making a highly technical comparison of the paraquat and Agent Orange theories and rebuking the farmers for letting the dog get into it. I found the notes and decided just to carry them out to the lobby with me. I knew that whatever I said was gonna be scrutinized, and I figured it would save a trip back to the office to prove my point if I just took the notes with me.

I arrived back to the giant, sickly dog with notes wide open. I began reading them aloud to the group after having given the credentials of Dr. Bailey as the world's greatest animal toxicologist. The very first thing that was stated in the notes was something that made ol' Pink's head swell up: "defoliant similar to Agent Orange" was right there in the first sentence. He looked like a banty rooster strutting around telling everybody he had told them so.

I began reading the symptoms, the first of which was "may cause GI upset," and before I could get another symptom read, Pink interrupted.

"It did more than just upset them GIs. It killed a bunch of them!"

I just kinda giggled with the left half of my mouth and looked around to see how the rest of the crowd was reacting to that statement.

To my surprise, no one reacted at all. They were just nodding along with Pink and waiting for the next symptom to be read. I sure wanted to break down laughing, but it is hard to do when no one else even got it. So, I just continued reading symptoms, and we all went to work to save the giant dog.

Turning Fifty

I turned fifty just recently. Eeesh. I got out of the shower on my birthday and just stood in front of the mirror, trying to see what twenty-four years of being a veterinarian had done to my body—the effects of working on animals that weigh as much as a Volkswagen. (I know you are probably grossing out thinking about me out of the shower and in front of a mirror. So am I.)

My feet . . . well, the left one was stepped on by a horse and has never really been the same since. The skin on the top of that foot peeled off and left this scar-looking patch that itches like crazy in the winter. Another horse stepped on my right foot, and now the big toe looks like a comma on steroids. The metatarsus that leads to it has a callus on the bone where the same horse broke it, but I just never got it fixed because I was too busy to go to the doctor.

My left knee bends both ways because I was trying to load a stupid racehorse into a trailer, and it backed over me. I feel sure that it's an injury that professional football players would have surgery on but, once again, I was just too busy. That left knee stays swollen all the time; it's about twice the size of my right knee.

The horse kick to the belly resulted in surgery to put about ten inches of mesh over the torn muscles and hernia that resulted. But once again, I was so busy that I went back to work two days after the good doctor, Beth, put me back together to do a colic surgery. This, of course, resulted in a much more fibrous scar than I should have, but it has held together, so I just keep on working.

My gallbladder went to crap a few years back. Can't blame that on an animal, but it probably resulted from eating junk food every day for breakfast and lunch for twenty-four years because I was too busy to stop and eat right. Gallbladder surgery left a series of scars that look like a smiley face with just one eye.

That neuro exam on a two-year-old horse left my right thumb broken, and it will now only bend toward the palm. For about a year, I had to use my left hand to pull the bum thumb away from the other fingers, or it would stay there all the time. I went to the doctor for that one, and he wanted to do surgery, but I told him just to put a cast on it because I didn't have time to go to the hospital for a surgery.

I have many colleagues to thank for sewing me up multiple times over the years. I would get kicked or smashed in the squeeze chute, and they'd just plop me down on the couch in my office and suture me up. Both of my hands and arms are covered with scars from these episodes because I never went to the doctor . . . because I didn't have time.

My old back has been broken in seven places . . . not by a horse, but in a car wreck I had while driving to work. When the ambulance arrived, I told the EMTs that I would go to the hospital as soon as I got done with the surgery I had been driving to the clinic to do. Thank goodness, they wouldn't let me.

There's an eight-inch scar from the same accident on the top of my head. It's huge and extra lumpy because I got someone at work to take all the staples out instead of going to the doctor. I bet you know why!

My left butt cheek has a permanent dimple in it where a cow smushed me against a palpation gate and tore some muscle that makes up my now-barely existent fanny. The same cheek has a scar where another cow horned me as I was trying to run away.

My left shoulder has no muscle left on the back of it since I was bitten by a filly after her owner assured me that she never bit anyone. I have precancerous skin lesions and rosacea all over my face from standing outside day after day watching horses trot.

I have brucellosis from when I stuck myself with a strain-19 vaccine in 1991 on a big ranch in the middle of nowhere and wound up being sick every night about bedtime for twelve years.

But overall, I would say I am pretty lucky. I'm still going strong. I thank God every day that he has let me do what I love to do for so long.

— *Seven* —

Cowgirls and Old Women

Like many things, the definition of "cowgirl" has changed over time. I cannot speak for the rest of America, but where I grew up, women did not do much on horseback. They were most often cooking and cleaning and keeping the home going.

This has changed as each generation passed. I never saw my grandfather's sisters ride a horse. I never saw my mother ride a horse. But the days of women staying in the home on the ranch have gone. Women now are right in the middle of calf workings and experts at horsemanship.

This generation of cowgirls is tough and ready. They know horses as well or better than a lot of men and have become woven into the fabric of the modern-day ranch. It has come with the liberation of the modern world, determination, hard work, and trials. Some of my favorite clients are cowgirls. They are wonderful.

Old People

Doing the same thing over and over and expecting a different outcome is perhaps the definition of ignorance. I have spent my life doing that and certainly continue to do it even though I know that it is ignorant. I suppose old people have just had more time to do the same things over and over. It appears to me, that this repetition of life events results in a perspective that we call wisdom.

I guess it just happens that when a person repeats the same situations that life offers, a predictable outcome usually occurs, and old people have that concept down. They may not verbalize it or even have it grouped into an organized thought, but they know it. It's this view of life that comes from experience that makes me love to watch older people live.

———

My mother has entered that time in her life. She is seventy-four years old now and has endured all that life has offered, and somehow she maintains a personality that makes everyone around her smile. She is the last living person in my life from the big six—that is, my parents and both sets of grandparents. These are the people who give us our genetic view of the world and the ones whose reactions we watch as we encounter life. The fact that she is the last one left has given me an uninterrupted view of the way she sees things.

As I observed my mother this weekend as we all sat around the living room and doted on Lilli, our first grandchild and her first great-grandchild, I mused about how much of my world perspective I picked up from her. She has analyzed life for twenty-four years longer than I have, and it would do me good to try to understand how she sees the world now. I did this, without her even knowing it, by asking her questions about life in the middle of normal conversations. She would go off answering and filling my brain with her genetics and making everyone in the room laugh and smile.

This is the perspective that I am lucky she gave me. She can hold the serious and tragic situations that life offers within her and use them for the wisdom that it takes to carry on. Yet somehow, she has learned that tragedy and seriousness are best replaced by "happy." Yes, this is what she does; she looks for the smile in a puddle of mud, the laughter in gloomy air, and the wisdom of not taking herself or life too seriously.

Old people are funny; they have an appreciation for things that younger people often can't yet understand.

Stage Chicken

Some things in this life just aggravate me, occurring with no rhyme or reason, like a bad dream or a pimple. Rude name-calling is one of them, regardless of that old saying that "sticks and stones may break my bones, but names will never hurt me."

Mrs. Peterson and I were in the clinic's equine center, ultrasounding a tendon on her studhorse. He was lame, and we were looking intently at the flexor tendon, trying to determine how bad the lesion was and what we should do to make him better.

It was one of those rare, quiet occasions when it was just me, the owner, and the patient in the barn.

About ten minutes into the exam, a loud, rather grating voice bellowed out from some distance away, echoing off everything in the barn.

I was under this twelve-hundred-pound animal and could feel its muscles tighten as the scary voice struck its ears. The bent-over position I was in left little option for a quick exit. If this horse lunged, he was going to step on some part of me that certainly can't bear twelve hundred pounds of pressure. But, just before he came to full attention, I was up—happy that my leg was still in one piece and attached to my body.

"Hello in there. How is everybody doooooooing today? It's great to see you," this fellow screamed, like a high-pressure salesman in a late-night infomercial. His words bounced off the rafters.

I turned across the room to see a man who looked as if he'd spent the last ten years working at a carnival. His matted hair hung to his shoulders, his face was covered with long, stringy, thin hair—he looked like a mange-ridden collie dog, and his clothes were covered with stains.

My heart was still pounding, and I was feeling a touch of anger as I stammered for something to say that would reflect my anger without being too rude.

Before I could speak, he continued, "I represent the [XYZ] Beef Co—"

I interrupted him right there, before his yelling put the already agitated stallion into fight-or-flight mode.

"We are working on horses in here, and they're frightened by loud voices," I said sternly.

It didn't faze him. Instead, he carried on in the same obnoxious way.

"And I was just wondering if you might be needing anything today?"

"Sir, what we need is for you to be quiet and go away," I replied, just as the horse began to dance around with flared nostrils and wide eyes. I had passed the point of being nice and added a tone of authority to my voice.

He continued in the same loud manner, but his next words left Mrs. Peterson and me with our jaws on the floor.

"We have steak and chicken, and . . . f--- you!" he blurted out. The words rolled out of his carnie mouth as he turned and got back into a little white pickup with a freezer in the bed.

I caught the two-word obscenity, but somehow, my ears did not hear "steak and chicken."

I thought the man had just called me a stage chicken. I had never heard that term before.

Judging by the two words that followed, I guessed that stage chicken must be a terrible thing to call someone. I was furious that he'd called me a stage chicken in front of a lady! I had no idea what it meant but could feel my ears turning red with anger.

"That was so terrible. I'm sorry you had to hear that. I've never been called that before, don't really even know what it means," I said to Mrs. Peterson in my most heartfelt, apologetic tone.

But Mrs. Peterson had heard it correctly. She knew the man had said "steak and chicken," so she assumed I was talking about the last two words he uttered—the expletive.

Her face had a strange, almost twisted look.

"You have never heard that before?" she asked. "I thought everyone in the world had heard that by the time they were your age. I don't use that kind of language, but I have certainly heard those two words."

My mind went into overdrive. She had heard "stage chicken" and seemed to know it was a derogatory term. How could I be forty-five years old without ever hearing anyone called a stage chicken? Yet this nice woman assumed that everyone knew what it meant to call someone a stage chicken. I didn't want to compound my ignorance in her mind, so I just went back to work on the horse.

Shortly after, Dr. Michelle came into the room to help with the exam. She noticed my ears and face were red and she must have sensed my anger. In a compassionate voice, she asked if I felt OK.

"Did you just see that carnie-looking dude who was standing at the door, screaming at us to buy his products?" I asked.

"No. What are you talking about?"

"There was a man here selling something out of the back of his truck, screaming from that door over there. He spooked this horse and called me a stage chicken."

"A what?"

"A stage chicken. He called me a stage chicken. Mrs. Peterson said she has heard of it, and that everyone else in the world has, too. I guess I've been living in a vacuum all these years, because I don't know what it means, but it really ticked me off. This guy looked like he hadn't bathed in ten years. I'm not sure I like being called a stage chicken by someone like him."

Mrs. Peterson started to laugh.

She explained that he had said "steak and chicken" and that she thought I was talking about his last two words.

We laughed about it for the rest of the day. In fact, we still laugh and call each other stage chicken every now and then.

Tammy

Sometimes you just need to stop and think. You know what I am talking about; some moments in the practice of veterinary medicine require a tremendous amount of contemplation. It is during these moments that a little peace and quiet would be nice.

Lameness exams often evoke in me the need for contemplation. Unlocking the mystery of an upper-hind-end lameness in a horse requires some thought. I enjoy doing these exams, but I have been known to sneak off to my office for a few minutes to assimilate the clues that I've gathered in order to make a logical decision on what the problem is or how it should be treated. The more difficult the diagnosis, the more quiet I require.

Tammy is a five-foot-tall, ball-of-fire barrel-racer. She has some world-class horses and is a blast to be around. When she shows up with a lame horse, it is usually a subtle one that requires my full concentration. The problem with that is that Tammy is a talker.

When I say she is a talker, I mean this little gal can't stand a moment of silence. It is almost as if she has a pathological aversion to being in the presence of others when no conversation is occurring. She will see to it that something is being said all the time, and most of the time, she does it with questions. This means that I become engaged in the process of obliterating the quiet with her.

This particular day found me working up a very difficult lameness for her. I was digging deep into my gray matter, trying to piece together the clues of why her seven-year-old gelding was three-tenths of a second off. It just wasn't flowing. Every time I would begin to ponder the results of the last portion of the exam, she would decide that things were too quiet and hammer me with a volley of questions. Eeeesh!

The last thing I wanted to do was hurt her feelings by asking her to be quiet, so I began looking around for something that would occupy her for a little while as I thought about the problem at hand. She rambled on about some horse she had ridden ten years ago that had acted a little like this one when it occurred to me that her constantly moving hands were a vital part of her constant conversation. I began to wonder what would happen if I could somehow still those hands. Would it stop her talking?

As she entered the fifth or sixth paragraph about the horse from ten years ago, I simply handed her an empty syringe case. She never stopped talking or moving her hands; she simply accepted it and continued on with the story without so much as a comma. Next, I handed her an empty bottle of Carbocaine, which she gladly accepted with her other hand and just rolled right along with the story.

This was actually getting kinda fun. I began to wonder how many things she could hold before she actually looked down to see what they were. So I handed her a pair of hoof testers. This stopped the chatter momentarily. The hoof testers were heavy, and she had no readily empty hand to hold them. So she took them, placed them under her left arm, and continued with the story.

I maintained eye contact with her and inserted occasional head nods to make her feel as if I was listening intently to her story, and I just kept handing her things. Next, it was an earpiece from an otoscope that was sitting next to me on the counter. After that, an extension set, still in the package. Next was a digital thermometer and the case it came in. She was still going on with the story, but her tempo had slowed just a bit. It was now becoming almost impossible for Tammy to move her hands, which was obviously causing the conversation node in her brain to sputter a bit.

I stopped handing her stuff for a second to see if she would pause and notice all the meaningless things she was holding for me.

Nope.

Time to hand her some more. There wasn't much capacity left to accept things. She had arranged them in various places to make holding them easier but she had no idea what she was holding.

I handed her a package of 2-0 Vicryl, still in the plastic, then the pair of rubber gloves that I had just taken off. Still not enough? How about a three-inch-tall stack of four-by-four gauze?

This finally stopped all ability to move the hands. She now had enough stuff that she had to hold some of it mashed between her arms and tummy. When this happened, all talking came to a standstill. Still she never even looked to see what all I had given her.

A few moments passed with no noise coming from either of us. I just stood there looking at her. Finally, I could no longer maintain a straight face. She asked why I was giggling.

"Thanks for holding all that for me," kinda trickled out the corner of my now-laughing mouth.

She looked down and assessed what all she had taken from me. She started laughing, too. And pretty soon, we were both laughing so hard that others in the clinic came over to find out what had happened.

"I guess you figured out that I can't talk if I don't move my hands. Well, I was just getting to the good part of that story when you handed me all this stuff," she said as she started to set it all down on the counter.

"Oh, no!" I bellowed before she could empty her hands. "You have to hold on to all of that until I have had enough quiet time to figure out what is wrong with your horse. Then you can set it all down and start telling me the story again!"

Every time she comes to the clinic now, I greet her with an armful of meaningless stuff and tell her if she can't be quiet, she is gonna have to hold it all until I am done.

Etti

I believe the hardest thing one can do as a veterinarian is break into the horse world. And I wanted to be a horse doctor. In my first year after buying the practice, I treated ninety-six horses. Ninety-six in 365 days. To compare, last year, we saw eight thousand. But I had no idea it would ever be like this.

I had heard about the Berry family since I first arrived in Lamesa. They lived across the Texas/New Mexico border and had a huge number of horses. The husband was the rodeo coach at the university and knew as much about horses as anyone I had ever met. I really wanted to impress the rodeo coach from Hobbs, New Mexico, because I figured he would send me a lot of good horses.

The coach called me on a Tuesday and said he had seven horses that needed a good vet. Without hesitation, I told him to come on over. We would do whatever we could to make those horses happy. He replied that he would be busy, but he would load them and send them over with his wife. He said she would be there at about one o'clock Texas time, and he would appreciate a call when I figured each one of them out.

I was so excited I nearly peed my pants. This was the break I had been looking for, and I did not want to mess it up. I spent all of Monday readying the clinic for my new, first class client.

One o'clock Tuesday arrived, but there was no sign of Etti Bess. I was going over in my mind the conversation he and I'd had a few days earlier and wondering if I had said something to make him change his mind about sending his horses. Two o'clock arrived, and still no Etti Bess. I was beginning to think that I had really irked him. You have to remember, this was the PCP era (Pre Cell Phone), and I really had no way to reach either Bess.

Three o'clock arrived—still no horses. I was devastated. I replayed our conversation a thousand times in my head and just couldn't find anything about it that was negative. Two hours late usually means not coming at all, so I gave up and pouted for a while.

At about three thirty, a truck with a long trailer slowly pulled into the parking lot at Brock Vet Clinic. A pretty woman, about thirty-five years old, got out and strolled toward me. She looked upset and dismayed.

"You will never believe how terrible my trip over here was!" she said with absolute conviction in her voice.

"I stopped at the convenience store on the west side of Lamesa when I got into town to get a Coke. I parked on the south side of the store and went in to go to the bathroom and get a drink. Well, it seems I forgot to put on the emergency brake when I got out. Do you know how heavy a Ford dually and seven horses are? I mean, I never thought to put on the emergency brake. I guess the pickup started rolling. Well, actually, I know it did. And it rolled across the street. And then up into a yard. And then through the front wall of this man's house. And then into his living room. And through the living room and into the kitchen. And then through the kitchen and into the bedroom. But at least it stopped there.

He was asleep on the couch in the living room—you know, he works nights. But anyway, it didn't hit him at all. But when he woke up, the trailer with all the horses was in his living room. He said that was quite startling. I can see why. I never thought you could back a pickup with a trailer out of a house, but you can. Anyway, I am late because all that happened.

But I think everything is OK now. He was in his underwear. When I came out of the store, I thought someone had stolen my truck. I was about to call the police when I saw my trailer sticking out from the front of that house. So anyway, here is a list of what is wrong with the horses. Sorry again that I am late."

I can remember thinking how calm this woman was for just running her rig through a house. I went over to the pickup and found stucco from the house's exterior stuck in the grill and windshield wipers. I couldn't imagine being so calm after such an experience, but this woman was ice.

I have now worked on the Bess's horses for twenty years, and every time Etti Bess comes over, I have to ask if she drove through a house to get here. We've become good friends.

Ass Spavin

There are just some things that cannot be taught in school. Some situations cry out for more than learning and science. This was one of them.

All I knew about the woman was that she was from San Angelo and she had a lame barrel racing horse. I had no idea that the episode that was about to occur was going to require every ounce of tact I could muster and actually leave me at a loss for words.

Six bodies emerged from the bowels of the giant dually pickup that pulled a brand-new three-horse slant. I was guessing that the entire rig had cost about $70,000. Wow!

As I watched the unloading process from the back door of the clinic, it became painfully obvious that this woman was bossy. She had brought her husband, her sister, her sister's husband, and both of her parents, and she had a job for each of them. It was like a military drill as she assigned each one a task and saw to it that their task was done to the very last detail.

As I entered the scene with a handshake and introduction, she gave me a slight smile and then launched into a detailed description of what was "ailing" her horse. It seemed that her only complaint was that the horse was not running as fast as it had last year. In other words, it was about half-a-second slower this year than it had been at the same races last year.

While she had been talking to me, her "crew" had saddled the horse. She climbed on board, still talking as she trotted off.

No one else in the entire group had uttered a word up to this point. They gathered around and watched me closely while I watched the horse. It was as if they were trying to detect any change in emotion or expression, and it was making me a little nervous. They were so focused on me that I was startin' to wonder if I had a booger in my nose or something stuck in my teeth.

"How long has this critter been lame?" I asked as I wiped my arm across my nose and sniffed.

The spokesman of the group seemed to be the brother-in-law.

He replied, "Ha, that's what we wonder." I had no idea what that meant.

The pressure was rising as I discovered that I couldn't detect anything wrong with the horse. I had watched the woman trot around the parking lot for what seemed like ten minutes, and that horse had not taken a lame step. The pressure rose even more when the brother-in-law informed me that I was the fourth vet she had brought the horse to.

I was hoping they would give me some kind of hint as to what the other vets had said was wrong with the horse, but they just stood there and stared at me as I watched the horse. Not wanting to disappoint them, I finally stated, "Well, he sure might have a little bone spavin." I figured this was a safe guess; nearly every barrel horse in the world has some degree of it—an arthritis that develops in the hock.

As these words left my lips, I began returning their stares to see if my statement stirred any emotions. To my surprise, it seemed to rustle up a disgusted look on each of their faces.

The spokesman brother-in-law said, "That horse ain't got no bone spavin. If he has any kind of spavin, it's ass spavin."

Once again, I had no idea what he was getting at. Nine years of being a veterinarian and I had never heard of that one or read about it in any of the literature. Not wanting to look stupid, I continued to watch the horse trot endlessly around the parking lot. I began thinking perhaps it was something the horse had caught from a donkey. After all, ass spavin sounded a little mulish or even a touch anal. I was wondering if I had missed that lecture in vet school. The brother-in-law had said it so confidently that it must have been a term that the family had heard somewhere.

I was digging for some way to ask questions and gather clues without appearing uninformed. Finally, I asked, "Which leg is it in?"

To this, the brother-in-law stated, "It ain't in no leg. Tell him what the deal is, Robby."

Everyone gathered in even closer as Robby, the husband, began to explain the situation. "You see, Dr. Brock, my wife has gained about twenty pounds in the last year or so. We know that there is nothing wrong with that horse; it just can't carry the extra weight as fast. We heard that you were good at explaining things and hoped that you could tell her; none of us has the guts to."

All I could do now was look at her pronounced muffin top as she trotted the horse in circles. What page of my notes from vet school should I turn to for the answer to this dilemma? My mind blanked as my face became red.

Two hours these people drove just to put me in this situation. They were all afraid of her, and I was finding myself scared to death of her, too. What in the world was this bossy momma going to do when I told her the horse was fine; she was just too thick? "*That's right, bigun, you lose some tons, and this critter will be at least a half-a-second faster.*"

Thong

When I was a kid, flip-flops were called thongs. But these days, the latter term refers almost exclusively to a certain type of undergarment. It took several years, many raised eyebrows, and awkward stares for me to retool my vocabulary, but I eventually made the transition.

And, although images of almost any beach suggest the two go together like peas and carrots, sometimes they just don't mix.

She was about nineteen years old. I had never met her before, and after the embarrassment that was about to unfold, I wouldn't expect to see her again.

She came up to the back of the clinic, leading a horse while detailing a problem it had with a tooth. She stopped walking at the back door but proceeded to dictate a long history about the horse's speed, and she said that she surmised its decline in speed was due to its toothache.

She was a barrel-racer, and like the rest of them, she was greatly concerned with speed. But she was a bit different from the run-of-the-mill barrel-racers I had met.

It started with her wardrobe. It wasn't the cowgirl outfit that most donned. She was wearing a denim skirt, a lacy green, baby-doll shirt, a pair of flip-flops, and an undergarment that left very little to the imagination. Curious about how I know that? Keep reading.

She continued to tell me about this supposed tooth problem as I motioned toward the stocks so she could secure the horse, and I could start my exam. She continued to talk as she walked in front of the horse to change its direction, but her mouth was moving faster than her feet.

I looked down at the exact moment that the horse's right front foot landed on the back of her left flip-flop. This set off a remarkable chain of events, beginning with me lunging forward to catch her.

Denim miniskirts do not stretch; they just move in the direction of least resistance. When a horse is standing on your left foot while the right foot is already overstretched forward, that direction is up. The farther apart her legs split, the faster the skirt rose toward her waist.

I didn't have time to calculate the physics of it as I reached to break her fall, but the flailing arms and separating feet left little to take hold of.

The horse politely stopped when it saw its handler was in trouble, but it didn't move off her sandal. Her hanging on to the lead kept her from going down completely, but it might have been better if she had.

Here is the scene: There is a nineteen-year-old girl wearing a miniskirt around her midchest as she props herself on one knee and two forearms while keeping her left foot squarely on the ground, thanks to a thousand-pound horse. It looks like an impromptu game of Twister, minus the colored dots and happy faces.

I bailed out on trying to catch her for fear of taking embarrassment to a whole new level. We both froze for a second in that position as we tried to figure a way to untangle this mess. Finally, the horse took a step back, and she sprang onto her back and then onto her feet, tugging down on the hem of her skirt that was gathered around her chest.

What do you say to a perfect stranger who just rolled into a ball of near nakedness in front of you? Nothing. We just continued as if nothing had happened.

We did the work-up on the horse, and I treated it as best I could. She paid the bill, jumped in her truck, and I have never seen her since.

That might be the day that thongs and flip-flops finally took on two completely different meanings for me. And I realized there would be times when the two just don't mix.

Toot

I had been working on her horse for several hours, trying to figure out why it was limping. It was one of those really tough lamenesses that requires all the patience one can muster up and then some. Thank goodness she was a happy, fun-loving person who was interesting to visit with and anxious to help.

It was during one of those ten-minute pauses between administering a diagnostic nerve block and waiting for it to take effect that she decided to tell me a joke. It was some joke about kids and getting older, but I really don't remember the joke at all. In fact, I didn't think the joke was one bit funny.

But she did. She told the joke and began laughing and laughing. I normally like it when people laugh at their own jokes, but she laughed way too hard. In fact, she laughed so hard that she tooted. Yep, tooted. It was just me and her standing there, and she had just tooted in C-sharp. What was I to do?

Here is a brief recap of what went through my mind: *That lady just tooted. I am now horribly uncomfortable and have no idea what to do. Just calm down a second, Bo, don't change expressions. Let her make the first move.*

Maybe she thinks I didn't hear it? No, that was way too loud; all the horses looked over to see what it was. Resist the urge to step away from her, and don't breathe in for a minute or so.

Should I just say something now and get it over with? I could make a joke out of it, and she would probably just laugh along with me. Let me check out the expression on her face. That will tell me if she is embarrassed or ready to joke about it. . . . Nope, she does not look too joke-worthy right this second. In fact, I think she is turning red.

Oh my, I need to do something to make her feel comfortable. Maybe I should laugh at the stupid joke now. Maybe I should toot, too, and then she would feel better about her toot.

No, we need something else to take our attention . . . something that will just move us on to the next subject, and we can act as if nothing ever happened. Come on, Bo. Come on. Think of something to talk about. Any other time you could think of a topic to talk about in a millisecond. Why do you have to freeze up under pressure?

Suddenly, I could no longer resist the urge to laugh.

Don't do it. But that was an amazingly high-pitched toot that must have lasted a full second. You could have tuned a guitar off the purity of that note. Bahahahahahaha. No, no, no, just think about something that is not funny at all . . . baseball, cryptorchid pigs, fishing shows on TV, having to sit through The Nutcracker *last Christmas. Yeah, yeah, that's working. I am losing the laughing urge. . . .*

As luck would have it, one of the other doctors came around the corner and asked me a question. Oh my, I have never jumped on to a question so quick as that one. In fact, I answered instantly and even said I should go to the other barn and check it out.

I returned about fifteen minutes later, and everything was OK. She looked composed again, and we went right back to working up the lameness in her horse. Wow, what a moment.

—— *Eight* ——

Look for the Moments

I'm a moments kind of guy. I look for them, relish them, hold to them, and pass them on. I feel like my ability to find the moments of this life is a special gift that God has given me that I don't really deserve.

Not long after I graduated from veterinary school, A&M asked me to come back and give a talk on what the first years in practice are like. I have returned to give that talk every year since. It's all because people like to hear about the moments, and it's important to me to encourage them to find the moments.

So, I encourage you—like I encourage everyone—go out and capture the moments of life. Look hard for them and cherish the effects each one of them has on your happiness.

Lab Test

Labs. That's what they call those scheduled classes in veterinary school in which they teach young vets the stuff they're gonna do in real life practice. We liked labs because they got us out of the classroom for a while and reminded us of why we came to vet school in the first place.

We had all kinds of labs; we learned how to float teeth on a horse, how to put intravenous catheters in dogs, and how to palpate cows. But one lab in particular stands out in my memory as just amazing.

I entered the basement of the vet school with my lab partner and best friend, John Horn. We were always on time—for everything— but for some reason we were a bit late that day. We would always read our lab the day before to be ready for it, but for some reason we hadn't done that either.

So, when we rounded the corner and entered the lab, we were completely unprepared for what we saw. At first I was dumbfounded, and then I began to giggle, and finally I was mortified. This was a lab for collecting semen from a dog. I had never considered how one collects semen from a dog. I had done it in bulls and stallions, but it never occurred to me that I might have to collect a dog.

Remember, I said that at first I was dumbfounded. You may won- der why dumbfounded would be a proper first emotion. Well, I will tell you why. It seemed that the only way to get semen out of a dog was the old-fashioned way—by hand. Holy mackerel!

Here I was, entering a room with my buddy, John, only to find a tableful of girls from my class whom I had known for two and a half years, doing *that* to a dog. These girls were the most proper women in our class. I never could have considered a scene in which they would be collecting semen from a dog. Yet, there they were, just getting after it on that dog. And, remember, at this point neither John nor I really knew what was going on—we hadn't read the lab.

That led to the second emotion I described earlier—I began to giggle. To see the very prim and proper vet students engaged in their task at hand just struck me funny. And it hit John the same way at about the same time, because I could hear his familiar snicker devel- oping as I felt my face turn red. These gals were working it. They were all ugly in the face, trying to get this twenty-five-pound mutt to give them a semen sample so they could evaluate it under the microscope on their table.

Now, I realize that we were in professional school, and things like that shouldn't have been funny. But watching four prim vet students doing that was frickin' funny. I didn't care if they were wearing white lab coats while they did it; it did not look professional to me at all, and it just made me laugh. I didn't want to laugh too loudly, so I was suppressing my laughter, which led to those occasional small outbursts of giggles followed by an attempt at composure.

But the funny wasn't over. My glance moved to another table, only to find four country-boy redneck-type fellas doing the same thing. Horn saw them about the same time I did, and he nudged my shoulder and pointed.

There was definitely a different look on these faces. One guy "manned the pole" and the other three stood there red-faced and disgusted. They were wearing rubber gloves and palpation sleeves and had their sunglasses on, as if maybe no one would recognize them.

Horn was laughing aloud now, and this opened the door for me to let it go and laugh hard with him. These guys had a forty-five-pound blue heeler, and that dog was smiling like there was no tomorrow.

Remember I told you there were three emotions? Well, suddenly I entered the third emotion, *mortified*, because I realized that I was going to have to do that same thing. Eeeeesh.

John Horn quit laughing about the same time that I did as a woman from the back entered the lab with an old-looking beagle dog and handed the leash to me. She informed me that we would be sorry we were late because we'd gotten the last dog, Snoopy, and he was a fifteen-year-old beagle that had been through this lab about thirty times and knew how to make it last. (Did she just say, "make it last"?) She said that he had only two responsibilities in this world; one was donating blood, and the other was this lab. She went on to say that he liked this responsibility much more than being an occasional blood donor.

As I looked around the room for an empty table, I noticed that some people were already through and looking at the collected samples. Their dogs were gone, and they were about done and ready to go home. Man, we were just five minutes late; those dogs must have been easy collections. Our dog, on the other hand, looked like he was no adolescent rookie. He was giving John a romantic look and sort of strutting his stuff as we walked toward the table.

"I will get the dog on the table and get the microscope ready. You can do the stroking," came out of my mouth as I picked old Snoopy up and set him on the table.

"No way, dude! I will get the microscope ready; you ain't getting off that easy!" John replied as he wrestled the dog out of my arms and set him closer to my side.

"Maybe we can talk one of those girls at the first table into coming to get the sample. They looked like they were really good at it. Why don't you go ask them, and I will hold the dog?" I asked him while he stared at the rubber glove I had tossed to him.

"No way! I am not asking a woman to do that. I think you should just do it and get it over with," John replied.

"OK. Let's just flip a coin and get done with this so we can go home," I said.

Of course, I lost the toss. Arrrgh! I couldn't believe I had to do this to a fifteen-year-old beagle. And by now, everyone else was through, but they weren't leaving. No, sir! They had seen me laugh at them, and now it was their turn to get back at me. They were not going to miss my lab with the Romeo of the dog world, who knew how to make it last.

I went to work. This dog was the master. He would almost deliver, and then he'd realize it and relax all over, forcing me to start again. Everyone in the general area was laughing hysterically, and I was about as embarrassed as I had ever been in my life. Even the woman who had brought Snoopy out was standing across the room watching. I could tell, as she giggled at my misfortune, that she had seen Snoopy operate many times before. I couldn't help but think that if we were anywhere but in veterinary school, I would go to jail.

That lab finally ended after what seemed like forever, and with it came my resolution that I would *never* do that again. If my clients ever needed a semen evaluation on their dogs, they were just gonna have to do that themselves, because I was absolutely never going to do that again.

Ennis

Having a veterinarian for a daddy doesn't make you any more of a vet than standing in a garage makes you a mechanic. But my daughters get asked questions about sick animals all the time, as if somehow my going to veterinary school was genetically transferred to them.

Nubbin is buddies with Emili and her husband, Garrett. He got his name from an accident that claimed the end of his thumb. Nubbin is a farmer and a redneck. He's the last person you would expect to have a Basset hound.

One night he called Emili in a bit of a fizz because his Basset hound, Ennis, was making more noise than usual. Basset hounds make noise. And making more noise than usual means way too much noise.

"I don't know what is wrong with him. He just sits with his legs out to the side on the kitchen floor and howls like something is bothering him. Could you come have a look at him, Emili, and see if som'in' is wrong?"

So Dr. Emili and Garrett made the trek to Nubbin's homestead to check out the possible causes of the perturbed Basset hound. When they arrived, they could hear his howls from the driveway. Inside, they found Ennis just as Nubbin had described him: sitting on the kitchen floor with his nose pointed in the air, howling like a wolf. Ennis was in misery.

Emili went to work. She asked how long it had been going on. Nubbin informed her since early that morning. She asked if Ennis had had a change of diet. "Nope," Nubbin had to say to that. She asked if he was current on his shots, if he had gotten out of the yard, if he had been vomiting or had diarrhea, if he was coughing or sneezing, if he was limping when he walked, if there were any fleas or ticks, or if anything at all might suggest why Ennis had the blues. None of the answers turned up even a clue.

Finally, Dr. Emili began a physical exam on ol' Ennis. She looked in his ears, his eyes, his mouth, his nose . . . nothing. She began touching all over his back and evaluating his skin. Ennis was a mostly white Basset hound with a few patches of black scattered here and there. Nothing on the top of the dog revealed the source of his misery.

Finally, Emili rolled that critter over and began to analyze his belly. There was the answer, plain as day. Ennis's skin was bright red on his underside, but especially on his scrotum. Not knowing what could have caused it, Emili suggested that maybe he had lain down on something caustic.

To this, Nubbin replied, "Oh no, I know what happened. He always sleeps lying on his back. And yesterday I left him out in the backyard all day while I was gone. I bet he sunburned his belly and balls while he was asleep."

This, of course, started son-in-law Garrett laughing. And I mean belly laughing. Laughing to the point that he was unable to speak for ten minutes. Here is ol' Ennis the Basset cooling his sunburned scrotum on the kitchen tile floor, howling with either pleasure or pain to the point that Dr. Emili was called in to investigate.

"What do you do for sunburned balls?" asked Nubbin. "I can't sleep at night if he keeps this up."

Being the clever and fair-skinned daughter of a veterinarian, Emili didn't miss a beat in her response. "You will have to go down to the store and get some aloe vera gel and rub the skin of his scrotum with it, or he will bark all night!"

So now, I'm like Garrett. Belly laughing as I imagine redneck Nubbin rubbin' aloe vera juice all over the scrotum of a Basset hound named Ennis in order to find enough peace to sleep.

Whoops

The cat's name was Whoops, and it fit the rascal perfectly. He arrived in a pet carrier and would hiss and slap at the crate door if anyone even looked in his direction.

Most veterinarians will agree that there is almost nothing as dangerous as an angry cat: four feet with razor-sharp claws, a mouthful of piercing teeth, and lightning fast reactions.

Mother-of-Whoops kindly offered to leave the cat in his crate so we could get him out when it was time for his declaw procedure. That's what happens when you are a house cat and decide that the arm of the leather couch is a good place to sharpen your claws.

Whoops had taken to this hobby about a month earlier. Now that the couch was ruined, Mother-of-Whoops had ordered a new one. The claws had to go before it arrived. I don't particularly like declaw surgery—it seems a bit drastic to me—but I guess it's better than putting the cat to sleep.

Here's how we do the procedure: After we anesthetize the cat, we remove the claw from the end of each toe. We do it in just the right place to keep it from growing back but without affecting the animal's mobility. After the claw is removed, we close the space with tissue adhesive (a fancy word for superglue) and wrap the paw with an antibiotic bandage. The cat usually is back to running around the house within a couple of days.

Whoops's surgery went perfectly. We put him back in the carrier while he was still anesthetized to prevent another wrestling match. In about an hour, he was back to hissing at me when I peered at him through the door. You know a cat's on the mean side when he lies on his side on the carrier floor one hour after surgery and hisses at everyone who walks by.

Mother-of-Whoops arrived at the scheduled time to pick him up. I told her he did well and was waking in the peaceful environment of his carrier. She smiled as I carried his crate to the car, content that her new couch would be safe.

About nine that night, the phone rang. It was Mother-of-Whoops, sounding a bit worried. It seemed Whoops would not leave his crate.

She had placed his carrier in a room and left the carrier door open, assuming that Whoops would come out when he felt like it. It had been several hours, but Whoops had stayed put, just as he was when she picked him up.

This news alarmed me a bit, too. I couldn't imagine why Whoops wasn't awake and alert enough by now to walk. I asked Mother-of-Whoops to meet me at the clinic.

She handed the crate to me and sat in the waiting room. I took the carrier into the exam room and opened the door. There he was, hissing and still in the position I had left him in hours earlier.

What could be wrong?

I had never heard of a cat being paralyzed from a declaw surgery. Everything had gone well. . . .

Then it dawned on me. The tissue adhesive I'd used to close the surgical sites had sprayed a bit when I opened it.

As I examined the hissing critter, it became clear that some of it had gotten on the cat.

Whoops was glued to the carrier floor.

I gingerly reached under him and cut the hair that was gluing him down. It must have been a larger explosion than I realized because he was stuck fast in several places.

He was up and moving—a happy cat—in no time.

I returned him to the owner and blushingly described what had happened. She was understanding and just glad that things turned out well.

All I can say about it now is . . . whoops!

Snakey

Growing up in the West Texas countryside, I spent most of my time outside. I had the opportunity to see, catch, and torment every kind of critter this part of the world has to offer. I have a pretty encyclopedic knowledge of West Texas fauna as a result.

One day, I was surprised to find a snake that looked like no snake I had ever seen. It was inside a cardboard box in the shed I was cleaning, and its gray body and large, rough scales were unfamiliar.

I'm not afraid of snakes. If they rattle, I stay away; if they don't, they'll probably just slither on about their business. This snake didn't rattle so I simply picked up the box, carried it outside, and dropped it on the ground, assuming the snake would take off, and I could then finish sorting the things in the box.

Not the case. The snake stayed put, even though I had turned the box on its side.

I thought it might have died in the box, but I wasn't about to reach inside to find out. Instead, I picked up a pig-show stick (a stick used to guide the pig as it is showed) and poked it a few times to get it to move on.

What happened next lasted only about five seconds, but seemed like one of those slow-motion segments in an action movie: I poked the snake and it came out of that box like a bolt of lightning. It must have been seven feet long and seemed to be the evilest creature I'd ever encountered.

It moved so fast I could barely get a good look—until it raised its head about three feet off the ground and started right at me. It began hissing and spitting and moved so fast I had no time to contemplate what to do next.

So I did what my fight-or-flight mechanism dictated: I started swinging that stick like a hyperactive Zorro in a swordfight and screamed like a little girl.

What was this thing?

I backed onto the step of the storage shed and could feel myself stumbling. Oh no, this would bring me to eye level with the creature, and, even worse, I'd have to stop swinging the stick to catch myself.

About the time my fanny hit the ground, the snake turned and sped off faster than a dog can run. It disappeared into the bushes and left me sitting there with a speeding pulse.

What the heck was it?

The more I thought about it, the more it reminded me of a black mamba I had seen at a zoo a few years before. But what was a black mamba doing in Lamesa? Those things live in Africa.

I was beginning to wonder if someone had released a mamba at our house in retaliation for an appointment gone wrong. I regrouped and went in the house to tell the kids not to play outside for a while.

I wondered how I might contact Jack Hanna, because I couldn't think of anyone else who could handle a mamba.

I told Kerri, "I'm afraid the dogs may be dead in the morning. I think I just saw a black mamba in the storage shed. It's the deadliest snake in the world."

"You're crazy," she replied and went on about her business.

The next day, when I told some people at church about the snake, they laughed and told me it was a coachwhip. I had never seen one in my entire life—never even heard of it—but after researching it, I decided they were right. I am still amazed at how fast that snake could move.

So, I've added another snake under my "Run Away" list, and you should, too. If you ever see a gray-looking snake with large, rough scales, run. It may not be deadly, but it will scare you half to death.

Is That What I Think It Is?

One of the fringe benefits of working at a veterinary clinic is an occasional bit of entertainment. Animals can be just plain funny. You never really know what they'll do next. It puts some fun into our lives and is one of the reasons we veterinarians have the best job in the world.

The dog, a German shepherd mix, checked into the Brock Veterinary Clinic motel on a Wednesday to board with us over the Thanksgiving holiday.

The animal ate, drank, barked, played, and spent his days just like all the other kennel residents. Nothing about the dog provided a clue of what was going to happen on Monday afternoon.

All was normal until about 1:00 p.m., when the dog had taken ill and was vomiting.

This was a big deal. We don't like to see our boarders get sick, so Laura hurried back to investigate.

What she found made her come running, face blushed, into the clinic to get the rest of us.

She announced that the German shepherd had coughed up something in his cage, and we all needed to have a look.

I couldn't imagine what a dog would disgorge that would make her blush, but I was about to find out.

On the way, I wondered what the animal could have ingested; it had to be something he swallowed during his stay with us. Whatever it was, it had put the strangest look on Laura's face.

We rounded the corner and could see the dog looking through the cage door, as happy and content as could be. No sign of depression or any other indication that he didn't feel well. In fact, by this time, he was wagging his tail and seemed excited to see us. I couldn't wait to see what had caused the commotion.

Then, there it was: a pair of red thong panties.

How could this be? There wasn't a tooth mark or tear on it. He must have swallowed the thong whole. It had been in his stomach for at least five days, when his system finally rejected it just a few hours before he was scheduled to go home.

Wow.

I've seen dogs bring up that red rind from around a slice of bologna, toy soldiers, milk cartons, paper towels, watermelon seeds, candy-bar wrappers, ponytail holders, nuts, bolts, and an entire cat.

But I never would have believed that a dog could, or would, swallow a red thong, hold it in his stomach for five days, and then toss it up in mint condition.

I couldn't decide whether I should tell the owner when she came to pick up her dog.

We decided just to put the item in a plastic bag and ask if she wanted it back.

She, of course, did not.

Boogers

A mixed-animal veterinary clinic holds a large number of distractions for the casual observer.

Many clients, just passing through with a pet or a large animal that needs attention, don't spend enough time with us to become used to all the clinic sights, sounds, and smells—or to the doctor's mannerisms. So, any number of small things can distract them while you are trying to describe what's wrong with their animal.

For example, there's nothing worse than giving a long explanation about how to medicate a pet at home, only to discover later that an unsightly particle of debris in your nose probably hypnotized the client half the time you were talking.

That's why we developed a "booger" signal among our staff. It's just a subtle change in facial expression, followed by a mock scratching of the right or left nostril to alert the offender.

The way our clinic is set up, you have to go through the waiting room to get suture material from one of the exam rooms.

This particular day, I was about halfway through a C-section on a cow when I ran out of suture. The palpation sleeves I was wearing were covered in blood and guck all the way to my shoulders as I made a mad dash from the cattle chute to get a spool of suture.

As luck would have it, I encountered a very short woman at the waiting-room entrance. She had a question, and it was very apparent that she was going to ask it *right then*. She pulled me over, blood-covered as I was, and started firing questions about her dog.

I was in a real hurry to get back to the wide-open cow, and assumed that she could tell that I was in the middle of surgery, but she was only interested in getting her questions answered and paid no attention to the blood dripping down the sleeves and front of my coveralls.

I caught sight of Berenda, our office manager, standing off to one side. For a split second, my attention left the rapid-fire questions and focused on her.

Berenda was making the booger signal.

The woman with the questions was perhaps five feet tall. I stand about six feet. This meant that she had a clear and unobstructed view into my nostrils. She was so short that no amount of head bowing on my part was going to obscure her view. And, with my hands and arms covered to the shoulders with the cow's fluids, I couldn't wipe my nose or even brush it against my shoulder.

Berenda seemed to find my predicament amusing. Out of the corner of my eye, I saw her laughing as I moved from one awkward position to another, trying to find one that would allow me to look at the woman without exposing too much of my nose.

She would shake her head each time I moved my head, as if to alert me that the booger was still visible to the client.

Finally, the woman finished with her questions and left.

Berenda was hysterical. "You don't have a booger," she said. "You just happened to look over as I was scratching my nose. You mistook that for the signal, and I didn't know how to call it off. Maybe we need another signal to cancel out the accidental one."

I have to wonder if she just wanted to see me go through the eleven basic ballet movements of trying to hide my nose without being able to touch it.

Persnickety

The dictionary defines persnickety as "placing too much emphasis on trivial or minor details." I have been practicing veterinary medicine for twenty years, and through that window of time, my definition of "minor details" has changed.

I have quoted the life cycle of heartworm and the pathogenesis of navicular disease so many times that I am bored to death with it. As far as I am concerned, the details are trivial, and I could do with never reciting them again. But most people have never heard those stories, and the diagnoses are not minor to them.

But it is not that type of minor detail that drives me nuts; it is that client who comes in with a list. Oh boy, do I ever hate lists. When I see a client pull out a list, I just want to prolapse. I know that there is gonna be a twenty-minute question-and-answer session, and that every answer I give will be researched on the Internet and queried among the checkers at PetSmart and the bag loaders at the feed store.

For example, one list-bearing banker dude is the epitome of persnickety. I dispensed some antibiotic tablets to be given twice a day to his dog. He called me up the next day.

"Yes, ahhhh, Dr. Brock, ahhhh, I was just calling with a question on the dosing of the antibiotic you sent home for my poodle yesterday. I hate to be a stickler, but according to the dosage schedule on the manufacturer's website, ahhhh, Missy should be getting thirteen-thirty-seconds of a tablet twice a day, and I believe you had us giving her half a tablet."

What!? Are you kiddin' me? I am talking to a banker about drug calculations, and he is correcting me? This guy got on the Internet, found the website, got the dosage schedule, calculated the dose, and came up with a fraction of a tablet that has the numbers thirteen and thirty-two in it?

I started to justify my "overdosage" by using some big, medical diatribe and trumping his Internet with my education. But, I decided to play along. I just told him to hang on a minute while I recalculated the dose. I then proceeded to tell him that he was correct and that he needed to break each tablet into thirty-two equally sized portions and then give the dog thirteen of those portions twice a day. I apologized for being off a bit in my calculation and said that the slight overdose was not dangerous to the dog in any way. But, I went on, it is very important that each of the thirty-two portions be exactly the same size.

There was a long moment of quiet as he absorbed the instructions. I wasn't sure what was going through his mind, but I was on the edge of my seat waiting for him to respond.

What prompts a person to hang on to such a detail? Had he not even considered for a minute the absurdity of trying to cut a tablet into thirty-two pieces? Did he just want to call and show me how smart he was, or did he actually think that I was an idiot who could not calculate a dose?

Instead of admitting defeat, he replied, "How would one go about breaking one of those small tablets into thirty-two equal portions?"

"I have no idea. Maybe you should just break it in half and pretend that six thirty-seconds of the thing flaked off when it broke," I replied.

This made him laugh. He laughed and laughed until I was beginning to get uncomfortable.

Finally, after what seemed like a good two minutes of fake-sounding laughter, he replied, "I guess that brings us right back to where we started. Wow, I guess that is why I am a banker and not a doctor, huh?"

You got that right, you persnickety rascal, I thought as he began another round of strange laughter. I had just spent ten minutes on the phone because of too much emphasis on minor, or trivial, details.

Pathology and Spiders

I sat there, looking at that computer screen, thinking, *How in the world can this thing be full?* The worst of all nightmares had struck Brock Veterinary Clinic, and during the process of trying to repair the damage, the screen came up with a message telling me that my memory was full. Boy, did this complicate an already disastrous problem!

I sat in the third row, watching a herd of three- and four-year-old children sing songs under the perfect orchestration of Ms. Young. I couldn't help but admire her infinite patience and gift with little kids. The third song in the second set flooded my brain with thoughts of being a child and this concept of full memories.

I sat in my study chair on the second floor of a rented duplex in Bryan, Texas, in 1987, studying for the last final of my sophomore year of veterinary school. Things were just not clicking. If you have ever gone through one of those marathon study sessions, then you know the feeling. I was studying for my seventh comprehensive final in as many days. To make matters worse, the subject was pathology. Man, it was dry.

You might be wondering what computers, singing children, and second-year pathology have in common. Well, let's go back to that night in 1987, and I'll see if I can put it all together.

Kerri's voice snapped me awake from a too-much-studying daze as she opened the door to the upstairs room. "Why in the world are you singing that song?" she asked as I returned to a conscious state.

"I don't know," I managed to say as I pondered the question myself.

"You have lost your mind. It is a good thing you are almost through with finals; I think your brain is full," she said as she turned and left the room.

The more I pondered it, the more I thought she might be right. I had not thought of that song in years. In fact, it had not entered my mind since I was a little bitty boy. Why in the world had I started singing it in the middle of studying about infarcts? I was beginning to think that my brain really was full, and it was looking around for information that had not been used in years to move to the recycle bin.

I ran down the steps and told Kerri my theory. She just gave me a look that said I'd confirmed her suspicion: I had lost my mind. She told me she was going to bed.

Back up the stairs I went and somehow found room to shove the rest of the infarct story into my brain, which I figured must have enough room to hold the rest of my second-semester pathology.

This sudden ejection of useless memories had happened to me several times over the course of veterinary school, but none of the experiences was as vivid as the first time I realized that my brain would hold only so much, and that it had become full on that night in May.

———

The third song of the choral set was "The Itsy Bitsy Spider," and this was the very song that had been ejected from my brain that night in Bryan. As I heard twenty kids sing it aloud, all of the information about infarcts that I had stored on my hard drive trickled out of my brain and bounced across the floor of the gym at the First Baptist Church.

If you ever show up at the Brock Veterinary Clinic with an animal and find me suddenly breaking out in "The Itsy Bitsy Spider," then you can feel sure that your animal has an infarct. I've determined that "The Itsy Bitsy Spider" is much more fun than pathology.

Tripod

The leg was broken beyond repair.

It is amazing the trauma that can occur when a dog is struck by a car. What made it even worse was the fact that this heeler dog apparently had no owner. He just wandered up into a young couple's yard with multiple fractures in one hind leg and a look of despair in his eyes.

The good, caring people who found him showed up at my veterinary clinic with broken hearts and a request to make him a three-legged dog. It was obvious to them that there was no fixing the leg, and, without surgery, the dog would suffer and eventually die.

Dr. Smith, a remarkable surgeon in my office, got to work. After a couple of hours, the dog woke up with three good legs and a second chance at life. He stayed around the clinic for several days while recovering, and we all became attached to his gentle and happy nature.

It takes a while for a dog to get used to having three legs. What a confusing moment it must be when they wake up from surgery and look down to find a limb missing. I often wonder what they think the first time an ear itches and their brain sends a message to scratch, but their ear still itches.

On their first trip outside after such surgery, male dogs usually spend some time looking at the now-missing leg and a tree that needs marking. Their faces take on a puzzled look, and the dance begins.

They move from one side to the other, trying to figure out how this new situation is going to affect one of their proudest moments.

But this heeler dog took to three legs like a duck to water. In no time, he was bouncing around the clinic looking as agile as he had been with all four wheels. As with most major surgeries, there is always a chance of infection because the animal doesn't know to leave the incision alone and often will lick and chew on the area. This dog managed to chew the stitches out twice, and each time we would go back and repair the damage. Finally, after a couple of weeks, the stitches came out, and he was ready to go back to his new home, now christened "Tripod," the luckiest dog in Lamesa.

It was sad to see him go, but we knew that his new owners would take good care of him and we would see him from time to time for vaccinations. Little did we know as we waved good-bye that his story was just beginning.

A week or so later, I talked to the owners. There was a little drainage coming from the scar as it healed, but otherwise, everything was going well. They just loved him.

Time went by. New patients came in; old ones faded into memory. We had filed Tripod in our memory banks, and were busy making new memories, when a voice on the end of the telephone one day gave us a surprise.

"You're never going to believe what happened," the caller said. "About four months ago, my dog ran away. I looked high and low for him, but finally I just assumed he was dead. He was the best dog I ever had. I just about had given up hope when last night he showed up at home and in good shape.

"Well, not exactly in perfect shape," the caller said. "I think I need to bring him in. He is eating and drinking OK, but you're not gonna believe this. When he left, he had four legs, and now . . . well, now, he has just three. Not only that, it has already haired over, and he barely has a scar. What do you figure happened?"

What kind of emotions must have been in this man's head as he experienced the reunion? How does a dog disappear for four months and then show up with a perfectly amputated leg? Well, we told him and we called the young couple who had saved Tripod.

Now Tripod is back in his original home and probably living the most amazing life of any dog in Dawson County.

Nine

Unconditional Love

I watched Ellen say good-bye to her horse. I watched from afar and wondered what emotions must be running through her mind. It is hard to say good-bye. People build bonds with the beings they love and almost never consider that the depth of their emotion is tenured by time and circumstance.

Wonderful things never last long enough and horrible things seems to last forever. Ellen was facing the reality that horses don't live as long as people. Neither do dogs, cats, or any other animal we let into our lives and love without condition.

As a veterinarian, I have witnessed this actuality many times. In 1990 when I began my career, I figured that time would temper the heartache it caused me when I watch someone's heart break. I was sure that eventually I would become calloused to it and behave like a professional. I have learned after twenty-five years that precisely the opposite has occurred; I have grown to be even less able to endure it.

I think it tells us a lot about the human condition. We were made to love and to care. We find comfort in seeing to it that life progresses in a happy manner and that we somehow have a part in keeping entropy from being the rule. Animals need us. We need them. We need them to let us love them and we need to feel like they will appreciate and long for the difference we make in their lives.

Sometimes I write stories and I can feel the laughter that I do my best to express. Sometimes I write stories to educate how veterinarians work behind the scenes to help people and animals be happy. And sometimes I write stories to convey that life is a series of deep emotions that must be felt and sometimes even cried about.

The wonderful thing about my job is trying my best to reflect the fact that all of those emotions somehow fit together to make doing what we do every day worthy of living and feeling.

Ellen cradled her horse's head lovingly in her arms as tears ran down her cheeks into the eyes of that sweet, sweet animal that had captured her attention for years. Time had run its course and the unchanging circumstance of death had seized the moment.

Ellen will be OK. She told me as she left that she would rely on the wonderful memories she shared with her horse to keep that critter living in spirit even after its body was gone. I found some peace for her in that.

It is this unconditional love and the bond of innocence that makes what I do a joy.

Randy, A Eulogy

Just this past Sunday, the clinic horse, Randy, passed away on his own—without fuss, next to his pile of alfalfa, and with his good friend, Elvis the donkey, standing by.

To clinic visitors, Randy was probably just another older horse standing in the back pasture, a sorrel-and-white paint with an occasional limp in his right front leg. If you went down to the pasture and looked closely, however, you would see that Randy had a lightning-bolt freeze brand on his cheek, that his limp was due to a knobby knee, that his blue eyes were sensitive to the sun and the dust, and that his feet grew into pancakes when they got too long.

If you had the time and inclination to spend time with him, you would notice that he ate his alfalfa much more voraciously than the grass hay, he actually halfway listened to the stall cleaner when he spoke, and he depended on his little buddy, Elvis, for security and fun.

Randy was an integral part of Brock Veterinary Clinic for fifteen years or so, after being surrendered due to a severe hoof injury. This eulogy to him was inspired by a single sentence Bo once spoke: "He taught me to rope."

In fact, Randy was responsible for the teaching of many. His initial role as instructor did, indeed, come in the form of roping. From what I'm told, he and Bo were staples at the rodeo arena, ropin' steers almost nightly for several years. Randy taught Bo to head (rope the steer around the head or horns). He also taught him what a broken tailbone felt like. They were partners, a man and his horse, both in it for the thrill of the moment.

As time passed, Randy's role transitioned. He became the go-to horse when the clinic got new equipment that needed to be tried out. He was an instructional tool for staff and veterinarians. That right knee likely had as many radiographs taken of it for testing purposes as all the racehorses that came through in a year's time. Tendons were ultrasounded as machines were compared. Randy even once had full-body infrared laser therapy as a practitioner demonstrated her wares.

Randy served the role of teacher to visiting students eager to put their hands on a horse and become real veterinarians. His saucer feet were nipped and rasped; his front limbs often abducted significantly more than seemed comfortable. Vaccinations were popped into his neck, sometimes vigorously and other times tentatively. His teeth were floated in fits and starts as students learned to manipulate the power tools used for dental work, and he always stayed sedated like a champion, rather than bouncing around as soon as the speculum opened his mouth wide.

Finally, Randy was instrumental in teaching me how to relax and let a day go by. Our evening routine, be it in summer, when the air was still hot at 10:00 p.m., or in winter, when fingers were too cold to buckle blankets, involved a large pan of senior mash for him to eat. Elvis scavenged whatever fell out of Randy's mouth, and I chased off the occasional extra horse in the pasture to ensure that Randy got his meal.

Those quiet times when the stars and moon shone bright, as they can do only in Texas, and the only noise comes from the soft sounds of a horse munching his feed, brought me peace that I can still feel. When I was at my limit from a string of busy nights with little sleep or I'd had a particularly frustrating day, as we all do, Randy's shoulder absorbed hot tears, and his dusty coat and pure horse scent brought me comfort.

In the eyes of many, Randy was just a horse. But to Brock Veterinary Clinic, he was anything but that. He lived a good life, and had an easy death, which is in itself a blessing. He is now buried in his pasture, with his buddy Elvis standing by, and will be remembered daily by the man who tossed him his breakfast, the intern who cared for him most recently, and the other vets as they examine ailing horses. He'll be remembered by Bo, as he leans against the pasture fence talking on the phone, and by me, now three states away, when I see a paint horse with a blue eye.

In my mind, his imaginary tombstone reads: "He taught."

by Emily Berryhill, intern at Brock Veterinary Clinic

A Tribute to Weenie Dogs

We said good-bye to the last of their two weenie dogs today. I felt their tears as the black one fell asleep for the last time. Nearly a year of poor health was ending, and with it came the tender memories that would be too sensitive to touch for a while. Some people would say, "It's just a dog," but I beg to differ, and so would the dog's elderly owners. Those of us who are younger may be wise to see how the sunshine years hold a tribute to weenie dogs.

The weenie dogs gave their owners something to care for—they were living creatures that still need their owners for guidance and the basics of life. Yet more than this, the dogs gave them purpose and meaning that carried on from years of raising children and grand-children. You can't just turn those emotions off as time changes its definitions of "parent" and "usefulness."

The weenies gave their owners stories to share with one another as the retirement years set in. Adventures hung in the air for hours, and short legs carried long backs through the mischievousness of puppy-hood. Each new trick was story material for the next phone call from family. Lap time was special; not a bump or change in skin texture went unnoticed.

And what about exercise? The black weenie was paralyzed in the hindquarters for almost eleven months. The surgery had been a suc-cess, and a good prognosis depended on a lot of physical therapy at home. Imagine that! Eleven months of walking . . . and exercis-ing . . . and moving those legs . . . and swimming that critter in the bathtub . . . and carrying it outside . . . and tucking it into bed. Kinda makes you wonder who got the most exercise.

This love is unconditional. So what if you go to bed at eight thirty? They'll be more than happy to stay right beside you until 5:00 a.m., when you start the next day. So what if you keep the house at eighty-eight degrees year-round? They've never known it to be different. So what if you drive twenty-five miles per hour on the interstate? They just love going for rides. So what if you tell the same story over and over? They just love to hear your voice.

I pay tribute to weenie dogs. I've seen their effect. I've laughed at those stories. I've helped you notice every bump and change in skin texture. I've monitored that exercise program. And I've seen that love in your eyes as you held your precious friend in your lap.

When the world has collapsed and there is no love at all, there will still be the love of a dog. They just don't know how to give otherwise.

Mouse Man

As a veterinarian, you just never know what your day will bring.

We had had a busy morning, and the afternoon was shaping up to be just as busy when our receptionist, Berenda, told me that I had a phone call. She said it must be one of my college buddies playing a joke on me. I answered the phone as I usually do and then just sat in the chair listening, as my mouth fell wider and wider open with amazement.

It seemed that the caller's pet mouse had a tumor. He was calling from a good distance away and wanted to drive to my clinic in Lamesa to have the mouse's tumor removed. Upon further questioning, it turned out that this individual had several pet mice, about a hundred or so. But that wasn't all. He had no money and wondered if I would remove Rosey's tumor for free. He had already tried to "strangulate" the tumor on the mouse by tying some carpet thread around it, but it hadn't worked. When asked how big the tumor was, I was surprised to learn it was bigger than the mouse!

So, what would you have said? What would you have done? Would you have said, "Sure, come on in!" Would you have dismissed it as a college buddy's practical joke and hung up?

Well, for some reason, I said, "Sure, come on in."

I had never done a surgery on a mouse. I wasn't even sure how to sedate one in order to do surgery! And, I halfway thought that no one would show up. I figured someone was messing with me and soon he would call back and say, "Gotcha!"

But that never happened. In fact, about an hour later, the man and the mouse showed up. It was not a joke.

There was a one-ounce mouse with a four-ounce tumor in the

clinic waiting room. The tumor was so large the mouse couldn't even carry it around. It was on the mouse's head and it looked like the Michelin Man. It was white and undulating. You could see where the attempted strangulation with carpet thread had occurred. Other than having this mammoth growth, the mouse seemed just fine. Its owner told me that it ate, drank, and defecated normally.

With that in mind, we set about the task of figuring out how to anesthetize this critter. We decided the best and least dangerous way would be to just put the entire mouse in the mask that we use to administrate gas to large dogs. You could say we sorta made a miniature gas chamber. Manda, my technician, held her hand over the hole, and we turned the gas on. It worked like a charm. This mouse was now in the perfect state for a good, old-fashioned tumor removal.

We needed some tiny instruments to work on a mouse, so we used eye-surgery instruments. The surgery was going along just great, when all of a sudden, I heard an "Oh no" gasp from Berenda and Manda. It is the kind of noise that makes you stop everything you are doing and take notice.

I looked down at what they were pointing at, and there it was. It looked as if the mouse had developed a rectal prolapse while on the operating table. So, now I am thinking, *How am I going to fix a prolapse on a one-ounce mouse? It is hard enough to fix one on a thousand-pound cow!*

Let me recap the situation for you: I've got this person sitting out in the waiting room becoming more and more hysterical as each moment passes. I can hear him crying and talking to himself. I have a prolapsed mouse on the table and no idea of how to repair it. I'm 50 percent finished removing the mouse from the tumor, and it is bleeding profusely.

It was almost to the point of complete and utter hopelessness. I decided that I had to finish the tumor surgery, and then worry about the prolapse. The bleeding was too extreme to stop and it was proceeding well. I was trying to make the thing as cosmetically pleasing as possible.

We were just about to finish up tumor removal when the prolapse starting moving. That's right. It was moving and squirming. It was then we realized that the mouse was not prolapsed, and it was not a boy. The stress of tumor removal had thrown this little mouse gal into labor. She was having a baby. I was so tremendously relieved not to have to fix a prolapse.

We finished the surgery and sent the mouse home to finish her delivery. Her owner was elated. He actually gave me all the money he had on him (a dollar) and thanked me repeatedly as he walked out the door. As far as I know, the mouse is fine and still having scads of cancer-prone babies.

John

It was a normal Thursday evening when the phone rang, informing me of a colicky horse on the way to the clinic.

My own horse had colicked a few weeks prior, and with no one within a four-hour drive of Lamesa who could do a colic surgery, my horse died. I decided then and there that I was gonna learn to do colic surgery and save horses for people who couldn't make it four hours to a surgeon.

I had always wanted to do colic surgeries. They are very difficult and require a level of expertise that horsemen in West Texas had not had access to. Performing the surgery required more than a simple decision; it required training that most veterinarians are not willing to attempt. I studied and honed my skill for weeks to be ready when the next horse needed colic surgery. It was my mission to bring the best veterinary care to the horses of West Texas that veterinary medicine allowed.

Here it was. My first colic surgery. The horse, John, was sixteen years old. He was a therapy horse for disabled and mentally handicapped children to ride and establish the human-animal bond. Dozens of kids loved him deeply. I did not take my responsibility lightly. I explained to Jenny, John's owner, that I had not done a colic surgery before and that there were vets four hours away who were better at it than I was. She looked at John as he suffered and looked back at me. She didn't think John would make it four more hours, and said, "Do your best."

So, I got to work. I called in my technicians, and we brought our talents and hopes together to work a miracle on ol' John. It was incredibly tough. John had an enterolith (a stone-like mass) lodged in his transverse colon. That part of the colon is one of the few pieces of the horse gut that cannot be exteriorized to the outside of the body to be worked on. I found the blockage quickly, but I had no idea how to cut open that piece of gut and remove the enterolith without contaminating the entire abdomen.

I went to work, did my best to figure out a way to get that four-pound petrified turd out of there. I blocked off other segments of bowel with huck towels and lap sponges. Remember, I could not even see what I was working on. In fact, the mineralized turd was stuck in a segment of bowel that was about three feet away from the incision I had made in the skin of John's belly. It was a full arm's length deep in the abdomen, and there was no way to see it. I could only feel it.

I could feel the weight of all the children who loved John on my shoulders. I could feel everyone in the room watching me and wondering how I would get such a concretion out of the bowel of an aged horse without killing him with contamination. But there was no way I was going to give in to the pressure. Ol' John was going to live to be ridden again by those who loved him, and I was going to see to it.

I cut open the bowel and removed that four-pound stone (four pounds!) from somewhere so dark, deep, and hidden that it might as well have been another world. I had managed to remove the blockage, but how was I going to sew up an eight-inch incision in a piece of bowel that I could not see? Oh man, huge pressure.

I had seen Dr. Deyhle blindly suture before. He had showed me how to use my hands without instruments or eyes to guide me. I put more than fifty sutures in a piece of bowel that I never laid eyes on. I worked until my forearms were cramped and aching and then worked some more. Finally, I closed the muscle and skin of the abdomen. I had done what I could do. I told Jenny that John's fate was now up to God, and it was gonna be a tough journey.

I do about 150 colic surgeries a year now. I have done that many surgeries for many, many years. But John was my first. I watched him roll away from our clinic two weeks post-surgery and thanked God that he had lived. I'm not sure how he did live—there is no reason he should have. I was just beginning to figure out how to do that surgery, and I started with one of the hardest presentations there is.

Serendipity must have been manipulating that moment in order to allow me the resolve to learn how to do colic surgery and to keep that beloved horse alive. John went on to touch the lives of countless disabled. They learned how super neato horses are because he didn't die on that Thursday he arrived in my clinic. He touched my life, too.

I found confidence in John that pushed me to learn more and become better. I studied hard and worked tirelessly to get to the point that I felt confident, no matter what the cause of colic. It all started on that Thursday night, on a horse that was just too tough to give up. It was one of those moments that made all the difference.

I thank Jenny and John for giving me a chance to embark on a part of my career that would ultimately lead to thousands of horses not dying when, by all indications, they should have.

———

I posted John's story on the clinic Facebook page, and a few hours later I found a comment from Jenny. It is sweet of her to say, and it is why everyone at that clinic works so hard.

> Wow . . . have been wiping tears from this for an hour now. . . . I'm Jenny . . . John's owner . . . Bo is more than a small-town vet as you all know! He called me "Sunshine" and wished me happy birthday . . . even though it never was my real birthday! I can never say *thank you* enough for what he did that day! For you see . . . "John" was my main man! I had based my entire Angels on Horseback Therapeutic Riding program around his expertise! John, by the way, was actually twenty-one years old when this happened . . . Now that just makes Bo's story even better! No horse that age should have survived, much less been operated on in the first place. But when you have a horse you have been with since he was five years and gone through so much, you do what is needed to keep him alive! John was one of "those" horses that were one in a million! He knew his job was to help the kids I put on his back . . . He would respond to them unlike anything you have ever seen before! Hundreds of challenged kids rode him over the years. . . . There were at least two or three that spoke their first words on his back. . . . His perfect demeanor and gait allowed a young bride-to-be to walk down the aisle of her wedding instead of in a wheelchair! So many successes I witnessed over those twelve years of doing therapy. . . . That's why Bo knew what he had to do and did it with

such grace! What he didn't tell you is this was done way before he had his awesome clinic and surgery bays he has now . . . just red-canvas tent walls with some track lighting and some great buddies and volunteers that showed up in full force, knowing the hard task ahead. Oh, did I mention that it was December 17, at 11:00 p.m., and it was seventeen degrees outside! When Bo stepped up on a box literally to bend into John's belly, you could only see the top of his Cinch jeans. Everyone was freezing, but when he came out and up with this four-pound football, I thought it was a joke. . . . You all know how [he] jokes! But all I saw was him sweating profusely in seventeen-degree weather and rolling this "thing" on the ground. . . . That's when I fell to my knees and started praying harder! Not just for John but also for God to guide his hands on sewing him back up! I only tell these extra details because Bo is too modest, and that's why we all love him so much! He goes beyond the normal things and feels the customers' pain and makes you feel like you are his only priority in the world! I'm so glad he took the chance to start his colic surgery expertise on John that cold night! John did therapy another four years and he lived his life out on my family's farm in Petersburg under the careful watch of my brother, Sid, until his death at thirty years old! And it wasn't from colic . . . just old age! Thank you again, Bo Brock, for everything you did and for not letting John die on that Thursday!

The Little Red Pig

The little red pig was in a bad way. His rectum was prolapsed and dragging on the ground. He was limping in both back legs, and he had a mighty cough.

The owner brought the pig in and gave Dr. Smith its history; but he didn't want the pig fixed. He wanted the pig put to sleep. Dr. Smith drew up the correct dose of euthanasia solution and injected it into the vein.

Thirty minutes later, the pig was standing up again.

Dr. Smith took the pig out of the cage and gave it almost twice the normal dose of euthanasia solution and put the poor little red pig in a padded dog cage so he could leave the world in a comfortable setting. Thirty minutes later, he was standing up again.

This was unbelievable. Dr. Smith gave the little red rascal almost three times the prescribed dose of solution. Thirty minutes later, the hog was up and grunting like nothing had ever happened.

Zach suspected that this piggy must be special. So, he decided to fix the prolapse, treat its pneumonia, and hope the limping got better with time. His daughter number one, Jesslyn, was looking for a 4-H project, and he thought this critter might just be the one.

After getting the OK from the hog's now-former owner, Dr. Smith set out to repair this strong-willed swine. His mission was not an easy one. It is difficult to fix pneumonia in a pig that size; not to mention its tremendously messy prolapse; not to mention its sore joints from a septicemia. It would be a long, uphill battle for this pig to ever even grow, much less become a candidate for the county 4-H show.

Father and daughter set about trying to get the little red pig back in shape. The prolapse surgery went well, the pneumonia treatment was progressing with few setbacks, and the limping improved with each passing day.

"Dr. Dad" soon designed a physical therapy program and strict nutritional plan for the little red pig. Jesslyn went to work, spending most afternoons after school following the plan he'd set out.

The months of hard work had saved "Some Pig" from certain death and, by county show time, he had even started to look the part of "show pig." But still, it was Jesslyn's first time to show, and who could think that a pig that had nearly died three times would even have a chance?

Their jaws dropped when the judge proclaimed "Some Pig" was the champion Duroc breed of the Dawson County show. The Smiths had been so sure he didn't have a chance, they hadn't even thought to bring a camera!

On Jesslyn's first attempt to show hogs, she won with a piggy she had saved from death row, nursed back from three different, easily fatal ailments (not to mention three attempts on his life), fed him well enough to catch up with the other pigs that had never even been sick, and then beat people with more experience and who had paid hundreds of dollars for their stock.

Man, what a story!

"Have You Used Honey in a Fanny Before?"

"Pampered" was a patient I met early in my career. I've never felt so sorry for an animal in all my life. Who names a dog "Pampered"? I'll tell you who—people who are planning on doing just that. This critter spent its entire life being doted on and fussed over to the point that I think it had brain damage.

Pampered belonged to a sixty-year-old couple, Freeda and Dick. You know these people. Their precious dog required every ounce of obsessive behavior they could muster. Anal-retentive owners of little dogs drive me crazy!

It was a Sunday morning, about 5:00 a.m., when the phone rang. Freeda launched into an unbelievable string of questions. I didn't realize it at the time, but that call came to characterize my relationship with these people for the next twelve years.

"Dr. Brock, this is Freeda. Pam-Pam is sick. She has been up all night pacing and is distressed. I really need to take her temperature, and I have four lubricants I can use on the thermometer: K-Y Jelly, Vaseline, Panolog, or honey. Which one would you recommend?"

Do you know how hard it is to instantly spring from sound asleep to choosing a thermometer lubricant? So difficult, in fact, that I couldn't come up with an answer. I wasn't even sure if I was even awake! Freeda cleared her throat a few times during the extended pause, convincing me that my silence wasn't going to make the situation go away, so I started speaking.

So there I was, forming sentences before I was really even awake, and some of the things I said were just as much a surprise to me as they must have been to her. It was as if my brain had taken over in a weird, parasympathetic way and was having its own conversation with this woman while I listened. And my sleepy brain didn't mince words.

"You were actually considering using honey on something you are going to stick in a rectum?" My voice carried an overtone of disgust that I never would have taken with a client in a normal situation.

"Do you stick the thermometer in the honey jar or pour the honey on it?" I asked. "Isn't that a little too sticky a substance to be considered a lubricant? Have you used honey in a fanny before? Where did you even get the idea to use honey? Did your mother do that to you?" It was almost as if I couldn't stop asking her questions. She never answered any of them.

I was beginning to wake up, and the more awake I became, the more I remembered to whom I was talking. If Freeda even sort of perceived that she had done something to endanger Pam-Pam, she was going to come apart.

"Oh my God, I am so glad I called you," Freeda declared. "Dick suggested the honey, and I personally thought it was a bad idea. He did say his mother used honey on the thermometer, but it was an oral thermometer. Would it have killed Pam-Pam if we'd used it? I am just so glad we called." She hung up without even saying good-bye.

I, too, hung up the phone and rolled over to go back to sleep. My wife wasn't going to let that happen, though.

"Who were you just talking to?" she asked. "Did you just ask them about sticking something in a rectum? I thought I heard you ask them about using honey as a lubricant for sticking something in a rectum. Is that what I heard you say? Wake up!"

Ten minutes later, after explaining all about Freeda and Dick, I couldn't go back to sleep. I'm still not completely sure which lubricant they used, but I'm sure it wasn't honey.

Fat Dog

It seems like we humans just can't help it; we have a need to care for animals. It is this deep-seated need that makes our dogs fat. I'll bet three out of five little dogs that come into my clinic are overweight.

It is an honest mistake. The owners are just trying to satisfy their pets, but have you ever just stopped for a second in the dog food aisle and read the packaging descriptions?

Succulent beef and chicken

No by-products

Tender morsels of bacon and cheese

Beef stew

Tasty pieces of real pork

Lamb and rice in hearty gravy

Hamburger patties

No wonder we have so many fat dogs; they eat better than we do. But the fact is, it is not the dog food that makes 'em fat; it is the table scraps. Those tidbits and morsels that we just can't stop picking off our plates and gently handing to Fido add up to major calories.

So here I am, standing at the exam table, looking at a fifteen-pound Chihuahua (that's more than two times its ideal weight of six pounds), and discussing the health risks to an overweight dog.

This dog looked like a walking coffee table. I'm thinking that this would be the equivalent of me weighing about four hundred pounds when the owner says the common refrain: "She doesn't eat much at all, Doc." You can't tell me that I'm getting up to four hundred pounds without eating too much.

It takes skilled questioning to get the truth, and it's a challenge—like being a detective. As the conversation proceeds, I learn that the dog eats only a few morsels of dog food a day.

When asked about table food, the reply is: "We don't give the dogs anything from the table while we are eating."

All right, does this dog get any other food besides the few morsels of dog food a day?

"Well, I fix him two strips of bacon and an egg every morning," is the low-volume reply that fills the air.

Now, think about that. When you compare consumption by weight, this would be like me eating forty strips of bacon and twenty eggs for breakfast every morning. What do you think? Would that add a little more depth to my belly button?

Once again, I am standing at the exam table again looking at an obese dog. I have asked questions from every angle that I can think of to determine what is causing this poodle to be so fat. Even the trickiest questions find the owner still convinced that the dog has a problem with its hormones. She swears that the dog never eats table scraps or human food of any type. I am just about convinced that this may just be more than table scraps when the dog starts retching. After a few heaves, a blob of substance lands on the table. Further inspection reveals a few chocolate chips and some doughy material.

"I thought you said this rascal doesn't eat any human food," I said as I picked up the pile.

"That's cookie dough," she replied. "The dog just loves it. It's not food until you cook it, is it?" Well, what do you think? Is it food if it's raw?

Other things make it very difficult to discuss obesity with a pet owner. Tell me this, how do you tell a four-hundred-pound man that his dog is too fat? That's a touchy subject! You certainly don't want to hurt feelings, but dogs were not made to be fat. We humans can handle it much better than they can.

My favorite diagnosis for a fat dogs is "You are killing them with kindness." Owners don't mean to jeopardize their health; they just want their beloved dog to be happy. So, the next time you learn that a client feeds his or her ten-pound dog a strip of bacon or isn't sure that raw dough is food, remind them that too much of a good thing is just that, too much.

Chew

The human-animal bond is a strong one, and at times, I am amazed at what people will do for their animals.

I know people who will treat their pets to an ice-cream cone before coming to see me. I've seen painted toenails, dogs with pierced ears, a cat with a gold-capped tooth, dogs with rollers in their hair, many types of sweaters, a horse with a glass eye, cat bunk beds, various types of tattoos on pets, an artificial testicle placed in the scrotum to keep it from looking empty, tubal ligations and vasectomies so the animals can still have fun but not get pregnant, wheelchairs for paraplegic dachshunds, contact lenses for poor vision in old dogs, tennis shoes for hunting dogs, and the list goes on and on.

But I have never again seen anything like what happened a few months back.

The presenting complaint was that the dog "just can't chew food." The dog, a burly bulldog that slobbered continuously, looked just as healthy as can be. Just looking at the critter, you could not tell anything was wrong. He just stood there panting and slobbering all over everything in sight, just like bulldogs do. The little lady who brought him in was obviously in love with this rascal—the look in her eyes was nothing less than terror that he was not OK.

When I asked what the problem seemed to be, she just shook her head and said, "He hasn't been able to chew his food for about three weeks now." It seemed that the ol' bulldog, Bule, had been unable to eat for a while.

He certainly did not look like he had gone without food for three weeks. He was fat and sassy. Besides that, why had she waited so long to bring him in if things were so dire?

"Something is terribly wrong with his chewing mechanism," she repeated over and over as I examined the jowls of this spit factory.

The more I looked, the more it became apparent that ol' Bule had dislocated his jaw. When his mouth closed, his already naturally misaligned teeth did not line up at all anymore.

I was amazed. How could this fat critter have stayed so robust without being able to chew? He could lick, though. Boy, he could lick. His tongue was about four inches wide and must have been ten inches long. And he loved to use it. The entire time I examined him, he licked his nose and my face. No matter where I moved, he would stick that thing out and give my cheek a good bathing. By the time I was through with the exam, I had Bule spit in my moustache, all over my glasses, in both nostrils, in my ear holes, and all over my hat.

"How have you kept this dog from drying up and blowing away?" I asked as I pondered the condition of the dog.

"Well, I kept thinking he would get better on his own. When it first happened, I thought it would get better, but it just hasn't. I just couldn't stand to see him take a bite of food and then watch it just fall back out of his mouth. So, I decided that I would just chew his food for him while whatever was wrong got better. I would just chew the food myself and then put it in his mouth. Some of it would fall back out, but he was able to swallow most of it.

"It didn't seem to bother him a bit—for me to chew the food. But don't you worry, Dr. Brock. I know better than to feed him human food. You told me a long time ago never to feed Bule human food, so I chewed his dog food, hoping that it would have everything in it he needed to get well."

I was mesmerized by the thought of this little woman chewing every bite of Bule's dog food for the last three weeks. She must have chewed it for a while and then spit it back into her hand before she gently shoveled it down his throat.

I was just amazed. Do you realize how much dog food you would have to chew every day to keep a fifty-pound bulldog in good shape? Can you imagine doing that for three weeks? What must her breath have smelled like? Why didn't she just get canned food? I started to go get a bowl of dog food for her to show me her entire process, but I decided that everyone might just get sick watching.

We fixed up ol' Bule's jaw, and he went on to recover just fine. I decided that this was the greatest act of owner loyalty that I had ever witnessed!

Prudence

It was a lush backyard.

I mean it was really lush. There were trees, vines, ivy, shrubs, bushes, fountains, and a potbellied pig.

That's right, a small pig called this paradise home. She had everything a pig could ever want: a muddy wallow, soft soil to root in, shade, plenty of food, and all the attention a pig could want.

My mission to paradise was to vaccinate the critter against all the "bad pig diseases" that might sneak into the yard. It was my last call of the day, and I brought along my five-year-old daughter, Emili.

We entered through the house, and the owner took us to the pig paradise she called a backyard. I had to pause for a moment to consider how wonderful it must be to live in this yard. As I stood there absorbing the surroundings, my eyes found Prudence sunning herself in a mud hole. The muddy spot was framed in the ivy growing around the trees that lined the back fence.

"Is she hard to catch?" I asked, as I pondered how I would give three shots to a free-roaming pig.

"Oh, no," replied the owner. "She just loves people and will come when I call her."

I figured she would come for a belly scratching, but what was she going to do when I stuck the first eighteen-gauge needle in her neck? How would I hold on to a slick, muddy hog that could probably make more noise than a 747? But, I wasn't too worried. Prudence was so fat that I figured I could outrun her. Maybe I could just turn her over on her back like a turtle.

Sure enough, the woman gave a sweet-sounding yodel. "Prudence, come here, baby," she called, and the pig hopped up out of the mud and waddled toward the three of us. We petted her while listening to all the stories the woman had gathered over the years of keeping a pet pig in the backyard.

I gotta admit, the pig was pretty cute. She grunted and oinked as we scratched her hard-to-reach places. I finally decided that the moment was right to slip the first injection gently into her neck muscle, trying the "sneak it in while she's distracted" approach.

The moment the needle pierced her skin, she turned into the fastest-moving animal I had ever seen! Her reaction time startled me so much that I let go of the syringe. As bad luck would have it, the needle had gone in far enough that the entire thing was still in the pig.

Off she went, heading for cover of the forest and mud with me hot on her trail. Just before we reached the heavy vegetation, the syringe detached from the needle, leaving a one-and-a-half-inch hypodermic needle embedded deep in the muscle of her neck. This was a problem. The weight of the syringe would have surely pulled the whole thing loose from the pig, but now there was nothing to weight the end of the needle. It was in there to stay.

We ran through the forest, dove past the mud holes, tangled and wrestled with the ivy, and darted around the storage shed; this pig knew every avenue the yard had to offer.

I was quickly realizing that Prudence was not as slow as I had anticipated. I can still hear my five-year-old daughter laughing and saying, "Daddy, you look funny running all bent over like that!" and the owner crying, "Oh my! *Oh my!*" over and over.

Have you ever tried running full speed, bent over at the waist, while extending your arms? It is not easy, and I am sure it made me look like an even bigger fool than I am.

I decided I needed a new tactic. Running was not going to do it. What a predicament—a panicked owner, a lightning-fast pig, and a laughing five-year-old! I was determined not to let this pig get the best of me!

Prudence finally settled back down in her mud hole. But, when I moved toward her, she assumed a sprinter's starter position. So, I would back off a little, and she would lie back down. She had a good view of the entire yard from her position in the mud and kept her eye trained on me. I could see no way of sneaking up on her.

It was then I noticed a giant beach ball next to my right foot—Prudence's favorite toy. I decided to use it as a decoy. I lay on my stomach behind the beach ball and gradually belly crawled, behind the cover of the ball, across the yard toward the stuck pig.

Tension mounted as I approached Prudence. The closer I got, the slower I progressed. I had narrowed the gap to about five feet without drawing her attention. I could feel the sweat beading on my forehead as I anticipated my next move.

Finally, I leaped out from behind the ball like a cheetah on its prey. Prudence didn't have a chance to move. I grabbed that needle out of her neck and held my hands up like a cowboy who had just tied a calf. Cheers erupted from my laughing five-year-old and the stressed-out pet owner.

Regrouping, we came to a mutual agreement that the risk of Prudence catching a contagious disease in the middle of her backyard paradise was minimal and decided not to try vaccinating the speedy pig ever again.

Josh

Josh was a fuzzy gray dog with eyes that bulged out like Marty Feldman's, and an extreme under bite. I estimated him to be about twenty-five pounds and somewhere around fifteen years old as I observed him tucked under his owner's left arm while she stood in the waiting room.

She had that indescribable look about her that screamed "I'm a waitress at a diner," and her face was torqued into an obviously worried expression that I assumed was the result of some problem with Josh.

She stood there tapping her toe, waiting her turn to check in, holding Josh safely in her left arm and a white plastic Walmart sack in her right hand. At this point in time, I had been in Lamesa for only a few days and I knew almost no one. Every client who came in the door was the start of a brand-new relationship, and I looked at each one as a new friend.

When we met in the exam room, I went to work examining Josh. I took his temperature; it was normal. I listened to the heart and lungs; it was normal. I looked in the eyes, ears, and throat; They were all normal. I felt all the lymph nodes and skin; normal. All the while, the waitress-looking woman was jabbering about how worried she was about him.

I proceeded into the next phase of the exam—patient history. Josh was sixteen years old (I was close!) and he looked a little arthritic. I began quizzing his worried owner about symptoms.

"Has he been vomiting?" No.

"Has he had any diarrhea?" No.

"Has he stopped eating or drinking?" No.

"Does he cough or wheeze?" No.

"Is he stumbling around or acting crippled?" No.

I was just about out of questions and had no clue as to why she was so worried about ol' Josh. I was about to volley another round of questions when the woman reached into the Walmart sack, pulled out a grungy-looking stuffed bear, and handed it to me.

I examined it. It was a gross-looking little bear with matted fur. It looked like some low-quality, grade-B stuffed animal that came from carnie row at the county fair. I was waiting to hear how this stuffed animal had anything to do with the problem at hand, but she just stood there and looked at me as if I was holding the answer to the entire world's health problems.

Still not a word. Just a raised-eyebrow expression that seemed to suggest I had no idea what to do as a veterinarian if that stuffed bear did not reveal the problem. I began looking closely at it again during the uncomfortably long pause. Was I was missing something? Maybe Josh had eaten one of the button eyes. Nope, both there. I looked to see if it was chewed or torn. Maybe he had ingested some stuffing. Nope.

Finally, after what seemed like five minutes, Josh's owner began to speak.

"That is Sweetie Pie, the stuffed bear. Josh humps that bear two to three times a day and has for the last fifteen years. I am extremely worried about Josh because he hasn't humped it one time in the last two weeks. I am completely sure something very bad is wrong with him."

I released my grip on the bear—all except the tips of my thumb and first finger—and gingerly handed Sweetie Pie back to her.

What the heck was I supposed to do about that? Dang, in dog years Josh was something like a ninety-year-old man. I was not ninety yet, but I was guessing ninety-year-old dudes weren't doing much twice-a-day humping.

I wanted people to like me as a doctor and tell their friends to come see Dr. Brock. I could tell that the woman was not going to have any sort of respect for me as the new doctor in town if I didn't get Josh back to twice-a-day humping. I was scanning my brain for any information they had given me back in veterinary school that would help me out a bit here, only to come up with nothin'.

Come on, Bo. Think of something, buddy. You can fix this! Use your common sense if you can't find any science. These thoughts were rushing through my brain as I stood there trying to look like I saw this problem all the time. I was new in town and I wanted to make a good impression.

I had seen commercials for low testosterone on television, and all those fellas seemed to be totally happy after a few doses of the hormone. So I decided to give ol' Josh a little shot of testosterone in the muscle. Not so much as to cause any type of health problem; just enough to make Sweetie Pie look as beautiful to him as she had for the last fifteen years. I had no idea if it would help, but this woman had not bought my story about Josh being as old as a ninety-year-old man.

About a week passed, and the Josh's owner called. She was as happy as could be. Josh was humping Sweetie Pie as many as four times a day now. She informed me that I was the best veterinarian Lamesa had ever seen.

Good People

It is no surprise that clients take up as much and usually more time than the animals we treat. Consequently, clients become the topic of many conversations, both inside and outside of the clinic. Most of the time, these conversations revolve around the people who made us laugh because they, themselves, were funny or because they were plain idiots, or people who made us furious because they were overly demanding or, again, because they were idiots.

Unfortunately, the people who are often left out of the conversations are those who deserve to be in them—clients who display deep devotion and compassion for their animals and respect for the veterinarians' efforts to heal. Here are a couple of the many who deserve recognition and whose tales will, I hope, spark kind thoughts and memories of others.

Angel was a miniature horse that arrived at the clinic for colic surgery with her owner, Sara. Sara was a college student who, in her free time, used Angel as a therapy pony for children with major disabilities. During the surgery, and with a wide smile on her face, Sara regaled us with stories of kids who wouldn't interact with any species, human or otherwise, until Angel entered the picture.

The morning after the surgery, Sara arrived at the clinic with her grandfather, who had driven the six hours from Dallas to support his granddaughter. He was a well-educated and very articulate man, with a faint accent that reflected his origin in France and life in Australia.

Sara had to go back to school three hours away, but Grandpa stayed with us an entire week at the clinic. Every one to two hours, he would take Angel out to graze and walk, regardless of the summer temperature or time of day. He would stop and chat and inform us of Angel's behavior, asking intelligent questions in his quiet and kind voice, but always at appropriate times and never in an obnoxious manner. He also made a point of visiting with other clients who were bringing in critical cases and kept track of how everyone was getting along.

One evening, Grandpa exclaimed that the "best part of getting old was helping his grandchildren," and that anyone who went out of her way to help others like Sara was doing deserved to be supported in the best way possible. He genuinely appreciated all we were doing but, he told us, if he could help Angel get well by providing attention throughout the day, then he would stay as long as it took. While he enriched Angel's life so that she could go back to enriching the lives of others, Grandpa also enriched ours while we worked around and with him.

———

Marcus was a Thoroughbred three-day eventing horse brought in for colic surgery. With too much small intestine involved to resect, but tissue that wasn't nonviable enough to make a clear case for euthanasia, we closed him up and recovered him. His prognosis was grim.

Sarah and her daughter, Olivia, the seventeen-year-old owner, were emotional yet determined. Over the next three weeks, they showed up without fail every morning at nine and stayed until six in the evening. They popped open lawn chairs in front of the stall or pasture, groomed Marcus meticulously and loved on him endlessly, and always brought a bowl of sweet and salty goodies for us.

The most striking thing about the whole situation was that Olivia arrived petrified of blood and pain. Over the ensuing days, she became my go-to helper, holding Marcus steady for his new catheters and blood draws, twitching him while we refluxed, faithfully syringing Well-Gel and Bio-Sponge, and altogether overcoming her fears for the good of her horse. She trusted that we were doing what was best. Tears often welled in all of our eyes as Marcus rode a roller coaster of bad days and good days, fighting with us as we fought to help him. Ultimately, Marcus succumbed to the fate we feared, but not without creating a strong bond between Sarah and Olivia and all of us at the clinic, which continues to this day.

———

For many, being a veterinarian is not a career but a lifestyle. The hours are not set, the outcomes are rarely certain, and maintaining the line between investing too much emotion or not enough is fine. Angel and Grandpa, the Sara(h)s, and Marcus and Olivia represent those who make our choice to be veterinarians worth it at the end of the day. They make the triumphs sweeter; the losses more painful; and they are, without a doubt, worth talking about.

—— *Ten* ——

Leonard

Success in life is simply a ratio of what we coulda done, to what we did.

—Dr. Bo Brock, 1990

I had worked on Leonard's horses since they were eight years old. Now, as I approached the two geldings from across a field of West Texas clover, they were twenty-eight. Leonard was a crusty old codger who'd spent his whole life as a cowboy in Borden County. His wife had died the previous September. They'd spent fifty-five years together, raising cattle and living off the land. Their ranch house got its water from a windmill and they collected electricity from the sun and wind. Their lives were as fulfilling as any I'd ever seen.

This walk across the clover to catch the two old horses was bringing tears to my eyes. These geldings had spent their lives serving Leonard and his wife, and they both had worn out at the same time. It was time for them to be put to sleep.

Leonard had stayed back at the barn. He had his arms draped over the top rail of a pipe fence and his hat pulled down over his eyes so we couldn't see the tears streaming down his cheeks.

Dr. Emily Berryhill had come with me to the ranch. She was the intern at our clinic at that time and hadn't been around long enough to know Leonard's history, so I filled her in as we ambled across the field to catch the horses. I looked over and saw tears in her eyes. Emily hadn't yet seen this side of the gruff cowboys who come to our clinic—the side that cries when his favorite horse is at the end of its life. She was now experiencing it firsthand.

Leonard had arranged for a neighbor to dig a hole under the only tree visible for miles. The plot was the perfect place for these two old geldings to be buried—it was their favorite spot to spend the day. From it, they could see their barn and get back to it in a hurry, if need be. They could watch the cars pass on the county road in the distance. They could see the cliffs of the canyon to the west and watch the hawks ride the updrafts. These two critters loved to be in the shade of that tree, and that's where Leonard wanted them buried.

It's an awful job, euthanizing a man's best friend. All of the memories of rounding up cattle and the stories of how those horses had gotten Leonard out of tough spots filled my mind as we laid the second one to rest in that hole. My trip back across the clover field to say good-bye to Leonard was a long one. I dreaded seeing his wrinkled eyes filled with the memories of how much he loved his horses.

We came through the last gate and hung their halters on their hook in the barn. I patted Leonard on the back and told him it broke my heart for him to have to say good-bye to them but assured him that it had been the right thing to do.

He looked up from under his hat, and the emotion of twenty-eight years of friendship ending on that day ran down his weathered cheeks.

"I'll be to town in a couple of days, and I'll get you paid, Doc," he told me. "Thanks for coming out here and doing that."

"You owe me nothing, Leonard. I couldn't live with myself if I charged a man to kill his best friend."

"But you drove seventy-five miles to get here, Doc," he said. "I gotta pay you som'in'."

I paused and thought a bit. Experiences like this one are why

I dreamed of being a veterinarian when I was a kid. I get to work with the salt of the earth, people who understand the bond between people and animals. It's the essence of what veterinarians do, and it has nothing to do with state-of-the-art equipment or making money. I'd kept those horses happy and going for most of their lives, and I was a part of laying them to rest when their days were done.

"You've been paying me for twenty years, my friend," I said. "This one is on me."

—— *About the Author* ——

Dr. Bo Brock, DVM, owns a thriving, multi-species veterinary clinic in Lamesa, Texas—population 9,207—often referred to as "the middle of nowhere." His passion is equine medicine, and he is well known across four states for doctoring horses of all types, from prize-winning race horses to working ranch horses. Bo performs approximately 1,000 equine surgeries a year. He graduated magna cum laude from Texas A&M University and was voted equine practitioner of the year for the state of Texas in 2007.

In addition to his thriving veterinary practice and moonlighting as an author, Bo is an active public speaker and adjunct professor at Texas Tech University. He lives in Lamesa with his wife, Kerri, of thirty years. They are the proud parents of three daughters: Abbi, following in Bo's footsteps, is becoming a veterinarian; Kimmi is studying nursing; and Emili has given Bo his first grandbaby, who calls him Poppi.

Crowded in the Middle of Nowhere is Bo's first book. Its first printing has been ranked as high as #5 on the Amazon Best Selling Humor List.